A stunning selection of great international
photographs... An exciting, fast-moving text...
Here is the full story of the fifty-year
struggle that catapulted Russia from monarchy
to communism, from a nation of peasants
to a nation of power...

THE SOVIETS

A PICTORIAL HISTORY OF COMMUNIST RUSSIA

THE SOVIETS

A PICTORIAL HISTORY OF COMMUNIST RUSSIA

BY ROBERT GOLDSTON

BANTAM BOOKS • NEW YORK • TORONTO • LONDON

THE SOVIETS:
A PICTORIAL HISTORY OF COMMUNIST RUSSIA
A Bantam Book / published November 1967

All rights reserved.
Copyright © 1967 by Robert Goldston.
This book may not be reproduced in whole or in part, by
mimeograph or any other means, without permission.

Published simultaneously in the United States and Canada

*Bantam Books are published by Bantam Books, Inc., a subsidiary
of Grosset & Dunlap, Inc. Its trade-mark, consisting of the words
"Bantam Books" and the portrayal of a bantam, is registered in the
United States Patent Office and in other countries. Marca Registrada.
Bantam Books, Inc., 271 Madison Avenue, New York, N.Y. 10016.*

CONTENTS

THE PRISON
OF NATIONS

THE AUTOCRACY

He was a young man, slender but well-formed, with a quietly handsome face and a shy manner. He hid a receding chin behind a carefully cropped Vandyke beard like that worn by his cousin, King George V, of England. He hid a stubborn fear of the world and an all but total absence of ideas behind opaque blue eyes. He was devoted to the simple things of life: hunting, fishing, riding, executions, his family, drinking tea—and autocracy. His name was Nicholas Romanov and, through a Divine Right in which he firmly believed, he was Czar of All the Russias.

The monk Rasputin, a keen, if deranged observer of men, once described Nicholas as "lacking insides." But this was not quite fair. Whatever emotions the Czar had been born with, had simply been frozen long since by the fear and violence which stalked his crown. As a young boy he had stood beside the deathbed of his grandfather, Alexander II, who had been shattered by a revolutionist's bomb; as a young man, he had seen his father,

Unemployed subjects of the last Russian Czar, Nicholas.

The Royal Family—Anastasia, Tatiana, Olga and Marie surround Nicholas and Alix, with Alexis at Alix's feet.

Alexander III, sign the decree which sent another band of revolutionary assassins to the gallows. He had inherited an absolute empire, complete with prisons, secret police, oppressed masses, dilatory aristocrats and a huge standing army. Russia — all of Russia — was his private estate, and he was determined to keep it just that way.

In this determination, Nicholas was enthusiastically supported by his wife, the Czarina Alix, a German-born granddaughter of Queen Victoria, who filled the boredom and vacancy of her royal life with a fanatically superstitious devotion to the rites of the Russian Orthodox Church. So frequently did the Czarina absent herself from the public appearances which were part of her royal duties, so obviously did she despise the coarse manners of the officers and aristocrats who cluttered the imperial court, that many believed she was, in fact, anti-Russian. Furthermore, although a 1797 Russian law decreed that only a male could inherit the throne, Alix, over the years, gave birth only to girls—four of them in frustrating succession—thereby failing in her prime duty as a royal breeder. For help, she turned to quacks and mystics, until the royal palaces were fairly crawling with astrologers, spiritualists and other fakers. But when at last Alix gave birth to a son — Alexis born in 1904 — it soon appeared that the boy suffered from hemophilia, the dreaded "bleeding disease" hereditary in many of Europe's royal families. When doctors predicted that Alexis would not live past his eighteenth birthday, the unhappy Czarina was driven to ever more desperate reliance on her "holy men"—on anyone who promised a miraculous cure for her child.

But it was not only the pathetic crown prince who required help. The royal family, the aristocracy, the entire Russian ruling class needed a miraculous cure at the turn of the century. Idle, vicious, profligate and empty-headed, the aristocracy fattened like a leech on the life blood of the nation. Uneasily aware of the mounting hatred with which they were regarded by the people, perhaps subconsciously suspecting that their historical function had come to an end, the Russian ruling classes took refuge from reality in a life of extravagance, idleness and vice such as had not been seen since the days of Nero's Rome. They clung desperately to their dream world, and none clung more desperately than Nicholas Romanov. This, then, was the basic definition of that "emptiness" which so many detected behind the Czar's eyes.

Royal Family and Court appear publicly in St. Petersburg.

Peasant women, arriving in Moscow to search for work, carry all their worldly possessions on their backs.

The measure of this absolute ruler of 150,000,000 souls scattered over an empire which embraced one-sixth of the land area of the globe, was revealed in the diaries he so assiduously kept. Over years filled with portentous change, bloodshed and disaster, these diaries reveal a spiritual wasteland. "Walked long and killed two crows. Drank tea by daylight," was a typical entry. When revolutionary mobs seized control of Moscow in 1905, the Czar serenely noted: "Took a walk in a thin shirt and took up paddling again...Had tea in the balcony." Count Sergei Witte, the hard-headed advisor of Nicholas' early years, once wrote, "I wish it; therefore it must be—that motto appeared in all the activities of this weak ruler, who only through weakness did all the things which characterized his reign—a wholesale shedding of more or less innocent blood, for the most part without aim." Nicholas himself explained things more simply. "Whatever I try," the Czar of All the Russias confided to his diary, "nothing succeeds. I am out of luck."

An Imperial pastime—Czar Nicholas plays tag at Court.

Teams of women haul barges on the rivers of Russia.

ETERNAL RUSSIA

Out of luck too—as they had been for many cruel centuries—were the long-suffering Russian people. They had never known freedom, ever. There were disputed legends that once some Russians had been free in the medieval kingdom of Kiev—but even if true, that freedom had been snuffed out when the great Mongol armies swept over the land in 1237 A.D. The Mongols slaughtered entire populations in their path, razed cities and fastened a grip upon Russia that lasted for more than two hundred years. And the misery of the Mongol conquest was matched by the misery of the Russian reconquest of their own lands. Under the leadership of the Princes of Muscovy (basically thieves, tyrants and murderers), the slow and terribly costly campaign against the Mongols lasted until 1533 A.D. In that year, Ivan IV became Prince of Muscovy—and fourteen years later, he felt secure enough to proclaim himself Czar of All the Russias. Known to history as Ivan the Terrible, he and his successors fastened so tight a yoke upon the backs of Russia's people, that it seemed nothing could ever shake it.

In 1613, after a period of civil war, a nobleman named Michael Romanov seized the throne. His descendant, Alexei Romanov, issued a series of imperial decrees which divided and froze the Russian people into rigid classes. Peasants were bound to the land on pain of death; townspeople to their villages or cities. The Church and the nobility were declared closed classes.

The millions of Russian peasants, now forever serfs, were looked upon as something less than animals. As animals, Czar Peter I (the Great) used them to build his "window on the West," Saint Petersburg, in 1700. Thousands of workers died in constructing that monumental city on a swamp—it was said that for every stone in it, a man paid with his life. And it was as animals that Catherine the Great drove her vast armies of serfs to the conquest of the Crimea in 1768, and Alexander I whipped them to the defeat of Napoleon in 1812.

But as Russian power made itself felt in post-Napoleonic Europe, so western ideas of freedom began to penetrate the empire of the Czars. On the death of Alexander I, in 1825, a group of army officers tried to overthrow the autocracy and replace it with a poorly defined parliamentary democracy. Known as the Decembrists—from the month in which they struck—they were quickly and ruthlessly put down by the new Czar, Nicholas I. Frightened by this attempt on his throne, he loosed a barrage of imperial decrees which reduced all classes of Russians to semislavery. Schools, newspapers, the army, even the Orthodox Church (always a bulwark

Russia's wealth was in agriculture, though few peasants were as well situated as these robust farmhands.

of the most reactionary sentiment) felt the heavy hand of repression. But Nicholas I discovered that he could not pursue an aggressive foreign policy in a modern world by leading armies of uneducated, ignorant serfs to the charge. When Russia suffered a humiliating defeat at the hands of France and England in the Crimean War of 1853-56, it was obvious that changes would have to be made—not in the name of liberty, but of efficiency.

Nicholas I's son, Alexander II, made them. He liberated the serfs and eased state control of universities, newspapers, the judicial system and the army. Rebuffed in the west, he turned Russian armies east to the conquest of the Turkoman lands, the Caucasus and eastern Siberia. He tried to reorganize the ponderous imperial bureaucracy and bring a touch of modernity to Russian life. His reward was the bomb which, on March 13, 1881, ended his life.

By the last decades of the nineteenth century, the time for reform had all but passed in Russia. The liberated peasants, still held in bondage through debt to local landlords, continued to freeze, starve, suffer the lash for any protest, to wear sandals made from the bark of trees and to live in mud and wattle huts on the edges of the splendid estates of the aristocracy. The age-old, untold misery of their existence had gone on too long. It was not of reform that they dreamed, but revolution.

THE REVOLUTIONISTS

During the 1880's the revolutionary movement in Russia moved a long way from the reformist hopes of the Decembrists. In response to the increasing violence of Czarist repression Mikhail Bakunin, the great Anarchist leader, preached a philosophy of total destruction, urging that secret committees be formed devoted to personal assassination. It was due partly to Bakunin's promptings that a small group of Saint Petersburg University students made an unsuccessful attempt on the life of Nicholas II's father, Alexander III. The students were arrested and some were hanged. Among those who paid with their lives was one Alexander Ulyanov, whose death had a determining effect on the life of his younger brother, Vladimir Ulyanov, later known as Lenin. When young Vladimir heard of Alexander's arrest he commented briefly: "Then that means that Sasha couldn't have acted in any other way." Thereafter he devoted himself to a search for some principle of history to guide him to more effective revolutionary means than simple assassination. He found this

The Ulyanov family, Simbirsk, 1879 — Vladimir (Lenin) at lower right, his brother Alexander standing center.

Lenin, already balding, poses with other founders of the Petersburg League for Liberation of the Working Class.

historical principle in Marxism.

Marxism had been brought to Russia in 1883 by Georgi Plekhanov, a former terrorist who had seen the futility of individual bomb plots and now urged the organization of a party of agitators to lead strikes and to educate the Russian working class to its revolutionary interests. Plekhanov founded a party secretly in 1883 in the city of Minsk, to be called the Social Democratic Party, and gave it a newspaper—*Iskra* (the Spark) which, printed abroad, was smuggled into Russia in thousands of copies. "In Russia," Plekhanov proclaimed, "political freedom will be gained by the working class, or it will not exist at all."

Karl Marx and his collaborator, Friederich Engels, would have been amazed at Plekhanov's presumption. They had taught that before a Communist revolution could take place a great industrial development must occur, the middle-class owners of the means of production (factories, mines, etc.) must abolish the old feudal aristocracy and all its works, and a politically well-educated and large working class must exist. In Russia none of these conditions had been fulfilled. Indeed, Marx and Engels viewed Russia as the repository of everything that was most reactionary and hateful—the natural enemy of progress, and the last place on earth where a Communist uprising might be expected.

But Plekhanov insisted that special conditions in Russian history gave grounds for hope. His Social Democratic Party gained adherents, and by 1903 held an international Socialist conference in Brussels. At this conference

Plekhanov lost control of his own party to Lenin.

Lenin was born on April 22, 1870, into an upper-middle-class family in a provincial district far from Moscow. As a youth he displayed brilliance and cool determination. Despite police persecution of his family for the sins of his older brother, he won a law degree (passing the four-year course in less than a year and a half) from Saint Petersburg University in 1890. By this time he had become a confirmed Marxist. In 1895 he travelled to Switzerland where he met the exiled Plekhanov and became a member of the Social Democratic Party. Returning to Russia in that same year he was imprisoned by the Czarist police and then exiled to Siberia for three years. During his exile he married a young fellow-revolutionist, Nadezhda Krupskaya. In 1899, their term of exile over, Lenin and Krupskaya returned to Switzerland where they helped to edit *Iskra* and spent the next few years in poverty-stricken wandering. By 1903, already the acknowledged leader of the "young guard" Social Democrats, Lenin was ready to challenge Plekhanov for party leadership.

The issue which divided the Social Democrats in Brussels was whether they should develop as a democratically organized party or become a dictatorship of the leaders of the central committee. Lenin urged that only a small, secret, dictatorial and utterly dedicated party could cope with Czarist repression and lead the Russian people—he was against democratic organization. By a slim majority, and over Plekhanov's objections, he carried his point. On this basis his followers claimed to be

The Russian revolutionist as a young man—Leon Trotsky.

the *Bolsheviks* (in Russian the word means "majority") while his opponents were known as *Mensheviks* ("minority"). But in actuality, as later developments were to show, it was the Menshevik faction which was in the overwhelming majority in the Social Democratic Party.

Standing somewhat outside the Party quarrel in 1903 was a young Russian intellectual named Lev Bronstein, who called himself Trotsky. He had gone through the same harsh school of police brutality, imprisonment and exile as Lenin, but his views, while close to Lenin's, were slightly different. Arrogant, brilliant and extremely witty, Trotsky's personality nevertheless lacked something of Lenin's moral seriousness. As Edmund Wilson has pointed out, while Lenin identified himself with history, Trotsky identified history with himself. In any event, the interparty squabbles among the Social Democrats were interrupted in 1905 by dramatic news from Saint Petersburg—revolution had broken out in Russia.

23

1905

By the end of the nineteenth century, Russian penetration of Siberia had reached the Pacific Ocean. There its imperialistic expansion into Manchuria and Korea at the expense of the moribund Chinese Empire had aroused the antagonism of a newly industrialized, militant and expansionist Japan. Nicholas II, who loved to dress up and play soldier and who, under the influence of his fanatically religious wife really believed that his soldiers were bringing Christian civilization to the far-eastern heathen, paid little heed to warnings from the "upstart" Japanese. Accordingly, in a surprise attack on February 8, 1904, the Japanese fleet destroyed Russia's Far Eastern Squadron at anchor in the naval base of Port Arthur. Within days Japanese infantry was pouring into Manchuria and Korea, and the Russo-Japanese War was on.

The Russian people had no interest whatsoever in this war, viewing it, correctly, as just another of Nicholas' blundering land-grabs. But the Russian people had to pay the price. On the front, they perished by the thou-

The Russo-Japanese War, 1904—Czar Nicholas reviews an infantry regiment on its way to the Manchurian front.

The Japanese showed surprising, unexpected strength.

The listing remains of Russia's navy at Port Arthur.

Father Gapon and a city official with a group of striking workers in St. Petersburg near the end of 1904.

sands in terribly mismanaged battles under totally incompetent generals; at home, they starved when wartime profiteering, corruption and inefficiency cut off food supplies from the big cities. These miseries plus the age-old deprivations and hatreds were the last straws. In January, 1905, Saint Petersburg metal workers, led by a fiery priest named Father Gapon, went on a four-day strike. When this produced no effect, the workers and their families determined to demonstrate in front of the Royal Palace. Father Gapon wrote to the Czar: "Sire! Do not believe the Ministers. They are cheating Thee in regard to the real state of affairs. The people believe in Thee. They have made up their minds to gather at the Winter Palace tomorrow at 2 P.M. to lay their needs before Thee....Do not fear anything...."

Nicholas' response was to flee Saint Petersburg with his family for the palace at Tsarskoe Selo. Behind him he left a welcoming committee of police and Cossacks. On January 22, 1905, 200,000 workers and their families, led by Father Gapon, made their way in dignified procession, singing religious songs and carrying *ikons*, to the Winter Palace. They had with them a petition requesting an eight-hour day and a minimum wage of fifty cents a day, as well as the calling of a constituent assembly to draft a constitution for Russia. At a point-blank distance of fifteen yards, the police and Cossacks opened fire into the dense masses of men, women and children. They kept firing until the snow was red with blood. Five hundred people were massacred and thousands more wounded. Father Gapon fled to Finland and wrote to the Czar: "The innocent blood of workers, their wives and children lies forever between thee, oh soul-destroyer, and the Russian people...."

After "Bloody Sunday," as the January 22nd massacre came to be known, a whirlwind of strikes, demonstrations and riots swept over Russia. Soldiers and sailors returning from defeats in the Far East added to the demoralization. Peasants burned manor houses across the land, the Black Sea Fleet mutinied, and Saint Petersburg fell into the grip of a general strike. The revolutionaries received weapons smuggled in from America where Mark Twain summed up the American view by saying: "If such a government cannot be overthrown otherwise than by dynamite, then thank God for dynamite."

When the Social Democrats in Switzerland heard of the uprisings in their native land, they hurried home. First to arrive was Trotsky who quickly set about or-

January 22, 1905 – Father Gapon wrote: "The innocent blood of workers, their wives and children lies forever between thee, oh soul-destroyer, and the Russian people."

The famous "Odessa Steps" sequence in Sergei Eisenstein's film Potemkin vividly re-creates the brutality with which Czarist troops suppressed demonstrations in 1905.

ganizing the Saint Petersburg workers into a Soviet (Council) which won control of most of the city. In Moscow, Kiev and other provincial capitals, similar Soviets seized control. Under the mounting pressure Nicholas II had no choice but to give way. He issued a manifesto in which he promised land reform, judicial reform, the establishment of parliamentary democracy under himself as Czar, and a constitution. These promises were enough for the middle-classes who, although avid for reform, were frightened by the upsurge of workers and peasants. Middle-class support for continuing strikes and riots vanished. By the time Lenin and Krupskaya managed to return to Russia, the uprising, lacking leadership, and with the people weary of struggle, had run into the sands. The Czar slowly regained control of the army and navy. When Trotsky called for another general strike in Saint Petersburg, his followers were smashed with artillery and he himself was arrested and sentenced to many years' exile in Siberia. Lenin, leading the Moscow Soviet, was forced to flee back into exile shortly afterwards. By New Year's Day, 1906, the revolution of 1905 was over. Nicholas quickly repealed all his manifestos and promises. The masses and the Czar had met face to face—and the masses had been defeated. The Russian ruling classes settled comfortably back into their dream world. They failed to recognize in the events of 1905 a dress rehearsal for a much more terrible and decisive struggle ahead.

PRELUDE TO DISASTER

The Russian Duma (Parliament), which had been convened by Nicholas in 1905 under revolutionary pressure, was dismissed at bayonet point in July, 1906. Later that year the Czar appointed Peter Stolypin, Prime Minister. Stolypin, personally courageous and intelligent, embarked on what he conceived to be progressive measures. He undertook to sell state-owned land to the peasants, hoping thereby to create a class of rich peasants immune to revolutionary appeals, and he tried to inject some vigor, some efficiency into the government. So successful was his land program that Lenin, observing from Switzerland, warned his followers that the reforms "might force us to renounce any agrarian program at all." But Stolypin's bitterest foes were closer at hand. They were the rich landowners, the aristocracy and, increasingly, the Czar himself. Nicholas could never tolerate the presence of men more clever than himself—and the Czarina hated Stolypin because he blocked the appointment of her "holy men" to public office. On September 14, 1911, Peter Stolypin was assassinated while attending the opera in Kiev.

The illiterate monk Rasputin grabbed power in Court by means of his hypnotic hold over the Czarina and her son.

Later it was established that his assassin had most probably been in the pay of the Imperial secret police—the hated "Pharaohs" who ruled a private empire of spies, assassins, *agents provocateurs,* responsible only to the Czar.

But by the time of Stolypin's assassination there was already a new "power behind the throne." This was the religious faker Gregory Rasputin, a huge and coarse peasant who had abandoned his wife and children in Siberia to try his luck in Saint Petersburg. Brought to the attention of the Czarina, Rasputin soon established complete ascendancy over her, and through her, over Nicholas. It seemed that this gigantic, bearded monk could (probably through hypnosis) stop the bleeding to which Crown Prince Alexis was prone. So great was his influence that ministers were appointed or dismissed on his say-so, the Duma was convened or dispersed at his bidding and his advice was followed on all important questions of state.

The ever-present police spies did not fail to report Rasputin's private life to the Czar. "He returned today at five o'clock in the morning completely drunk." "On the night of 25th-26th the actress V. spent the night with Rasputin." "Rasputin came home with the Princess Sh— very drunk...." But such reports had little effect on the Czarina. She wrote to the Czar, "the Scribes and Pharisees are persecuting Christ....They accuse Rasputin of kissing women, etc. Read the apostles; they kissed everybody...." In actuality, the Russian ruling classes, with social catastrophe looming ever closer on the horizon, turned to Rasputin in search of that miracle which might save them. As a Czarist senator was to remark: "If there had been no Rasputin, it would have been necessary to invent one."

Meanwhile the revolutionaries, scattered in exile or suffering in Siberia, slowly rebuilt their organization. Trotsky escaped from Siberia by hiding under a wagon-load of hay, and made his way across Europe to Switzerland where he found Lenin carrying on his endless feud with the Mensheviks. Over the following years the Menshevik-Bolshevik split in the Social Democratic Party deepened and widened irreparably. The argument between them was basically over whether or not Russia was ripe for a Communist revolution. The Mensheviks, cleaving to Marx's analyses, held that a middle-class revolution would have to occur first. Therefore, they argued, the Social Democrats should cooperate with liberal parties in hastening a democratic revolution. But Lenin and the Bolsheviks held that because of certain peculiarities in Russia's historical development, there was no need for a middle-class revolution. When the people finally rose, they must be led straight into communism. To cooperate with middle-class, liberal parties would be to betray the workers and peasants. At committee meetings, Party Congresses, through underground newspapers such as *Pravda* (Truth), in countless pamphlets and books, Lenin hammered home his thesis. While the Mensheviks remained a large majority both in exile and inside Russia, by 1914 there were an estimated 30,000 Bolsheviks dedicated to Lenin's ideas. But in that same

World War I—Mobilized reservists arrive in Petersburg.

year, all the interparty quarrels and arguments were overshadowed by the onset of sudden European disaster.

Nicholas' dilettante and idiotic foreign policy helped to provoke the catastrophe. Despite the bruises his expansionism had suffered at the hands of the Japanese in 1905, Nicholas still looked on himself as the protector of all European Slavs. His policy of "Pan-Slavism" had caused him to guarantee the independence of various small Balkan nations such as Serbia and Bulgaria. In the summer of 1914, Serbian terrorists assassinated Archduke Franz Ferdinand, heir to the Austrian throne, in the streets of Sarajevo. Austria-Hungary issued a severe

ultimatum to Serbia and, despite Serbian acceptance of most of its provisions, declared war on the small Slav country. Russia immediately mobilized her forces along the Austrian frontier. Austria's ally, Germany, then mobilized her armies. But Russia was allied to France, and when Germany mobilized, so did the French. England had an unwritten understanding with France. And so it was the armies marched into World War I. Nicholas II, as responsible as any man for this disaster, not only helped ignite the bloodiest war in human history, but also lit a trail of gunpowder which blew himself, his throne and the entire ancient autocracy of Russia sky-high.

THE TWO
REVOLUTIONS

WORLD WAR I

The war came as a stunning surprise to the Russian people. Devoting most of their time to the great effort of simply staying alive, they understood almost nothing of foreign affairs. Yet, when the catastrophe of August, 1914, broke over their homeland, they responded enthusiastically. Ever since 1912 there had been a rebirth of popular strikes and demonstrations in the big cities. Now all that ceased. Internal hatreds were to be vented on foreign foes. On the day war was declared, thousands of workers gathered outside the Winter Palace in Saint Petersburg to sing "God Save the Czar," while other thousands burned the German Embassy. The very name of the capital city was changed from the German-sounding Saint Petersburg to the more Russian Petrograd. Patriotic fervor was such that Russians even accepted a government decree banning the sale of vodka and outlawing drunkenness! That this same decree cut off much-needed government reve-

Russian troops in a running attack against the Germans.

Russian soldiers at the front. Crowded trenches and the everlasting mud soon became symbols of the long war.

nue (the sale of vodka was a government monopoly), none seemed to notice.

And at first things seemed to go well. With the major German armies pouring through Belgium and into France, Russia loyally undertook an offensive against East Prussia, although her mobilization was not yet complete. In all the Allied countries men looked hopefully on the Russian "steamroller," which, though cranky and ill-equipped, would surely drown the Germans through weight of manpower alone. Two Russian armies advanced against little opposition into East Prussia.

But behind the façade of power existed a vacuum of leadership, an unbelievable lack of equipment, and corruption which reached all the way to the High Command itself. Grand Duke Nicholas, second cousin to the Czar and over-all commander of Russia's armies, knew nothing of modern warfare; his generals knew less. War Minister Vladimir Sukhomlinov, who boasted that he had not read a military manual in twenty-five years and placed his trust in bayonet and cavalry charges, was suspected of being in German pay. Thousands of Russian soldiers had no rifles; they were expected to rush forward empty-handed, picking up the rifles of their fallen comrades. Nearly half the troops had no shoes. Artillery, traditionally a Russian specialty, was almost nonexistent, as were munitions. There was a great shortage of field telephones, and as most commanders could not figure out the army codes anyhow, messages were broadcast in clear on radio.

The German army in East Prussia, under the leadership of the brilliant and energetic General Eric Ludendorff and the firm, if placid General Von Hindenburg, prepared a trap for the Russian armies and then closed

Czar Nicholas (third from right) appears with the other Allied officers in his new role as Supreme Commander.

it with devastating effect. At Tannenberg in East Prussia, two Russian armies were annihilated in one of the greatest military debacles in history. Yet, because the Russian advance had drawn off two German army corps from the Western Front, it had not been in vain. The Battle of the Marne, which saved France, may well have been won by the Russian disaster in East Prussia.

Against the armies of Austria, the Russians did better, advancing far into Austrian territory. But as soon as the Western Front stabilized into its grim trench-warfare, and German divisions and generals could be shifted east, disaster overwhelmed the Russians there also. After the first months of the war, despite occasional victories, the fighting became one long, agonizing retreat. A new War Minister, Polivanov, explained his strategy: "I place my faith in the impenetrable spaces, impassable mud, and the mercy of Saint Nicholas Mirlikisky, Protector of Holy Russia." His strategy was insufficient.

The poorly equipped Russian artillery goes into action.

A staff meeting at the Russian Headquarters in 1916. Russian armies in the west had retreated two hundred miles in only three months before the German attack.

By armies of hundreds of thousands, the ill-armed and ill-trained peasants were poured into the holocaust. Soon morale began to waver and then break. Despite floggings and firing squads, retreats turned into routs and desertion became epidemic. The Russian peasant-soldier was breaking beneath an insupportable load. Sir Bernard Pares, in Russia with the Red Cross, recorded: "I saw a regiment lose three quarters of its men in a few hours. I was present at another action where...every battalion in the front line was reduced from one thousand to a figure between ninety and one hundred. I saw an English surgeon, with one unqualified Russian assistant, deal with three or four hundred cases at a first-aid station...he had hardly any anaesthetic."

As military catastrophe deepened, the Duma liberals and the aristocracy, scenting revolution in the air, grew frantic. They bombarded the Czar with demands that the war effort be placed in more competent hands. In answer, Nicholas assumed the Supreme Command himself and

The debacle deepens—Russians captured by the Germans.

continued to follow the advice of his deranged wife and her mentor, Rasputin. "This must be your war," the Czarina wrote to Nicholas, "and your peace...and not by any means the Duma's....Bring your fist down on the table. Don't yield. Be the boss. Obey your firm little wife and Our Friend [Rasputin]...people want to feel your hand....Russia loves to feel the whip. That is their nature."

But as Russian armies melted away at the front and the big cities became again the scene of strikes, protests and demonstrations, a small group of frightened aristocrats determined to save the situation by murdering Rasputin, the "evil genius" of the monarchy. Their plan (which Trotsky called "a moving-picture scenario designed for people of bad taste") bore fruit on December 29, 1916. On that evening, Prince Felix Yussupov entertained Rasputin at a private party. He fed him potassium cyanide. In another room, Yussupov's co-conspirators kept up their courage by playing an ancient record of "Yankee Doodle" over and over again. When the cyanide had no apparent effect on the gigantic monk, Yussupov pulled out a pistol and shot him—then shot him again, and then again, his hysteria mounting as the monk refused to die. Finally, their victim probably (but not certainly) dead, the conspirators carried his body in a car borrowed from Grand Duke Dmitri to the Neva River and shoved it under the ice. They had, they thought, saved Russia and averted revolution. But Rasputin himself had long ago predicted that the monarchy would not outlive him.

With Russian losses in the millions, corpses were buried beneath simple wooden crosses in hastily dug graves.

THE FEBRUARY REVOLUTION

The misery brought by war reached new heights in February, 1917, when bread rationing produced long lines of hungry housewives on the freezing streets of Petrograd. The irony of the fact that March 8 was to be celebrated as International Women's Day was not lost on these endless and anxious queues. On March 8, the women workers in Petrograd's textile factories went out on strike, joined by the men of the huge Putilov metal works. They formed processions and marched through the streets beneath banners which proclaimed "Down With The Autocracy!" Despite police cordons, ninety-thousand marchers reached the Nevsky Prospect, Petrograd's Fifth Avenue. Before the Duma building they shouted for bread—a hopeless request. On March 9 the number of demonstrators doubled. And to the disbelief of both the crowds and the city officials, the Cossacks refused to follow orders to disperse the mobs. The crowds were immensely heartened by the fact, and by rumors which now swept through the city.

Propaganda being distributed in Moscow during the early
days of the February uprising, the first 1917 revolution.

A policeman had struck a woman with his club, and, it was said, a nearby Cossack had cut the hated Pharaoh down with his saber! Twenty-five hundred strikers from the Erikson plants ran into a Cossack squadron on Sampsonievsky Prospect and the Cossacks let them through! Kayurov, a Bolshevik worker, said: "Some of them [the Cossacks] smiled, and one of them gave the workers a good wink!" Evidently, the Cossacks, those ancient subduers of the people, were as sick of war and famine and repression as everyone else. The night of March 9 was one of hope for the workers. On the following day no less than 240,000 people thronged the streets of Petrograd. The police opened fire on them and were cut down by volleys from Cossack rifles. When a group of workers to which Kayurov was attached was attacked by police, he ran to a nearby Cossack squadron. "Brothers—Cossacks, help the workers in a struggle for their peaceable demands; you see how the Pharaohs treat us hungry workers. Help us!" The Cossacks exchanged glances and then charged down upon the police. On March 10 the police retired from the Petrograd streets and went into hiding.

On that same day, General Khabalov, Military Governor of Petrograd, called out the elite guard regiments. Towards these soldiers the crowds were more cautious. Women workers were sent to harangue the lines of sullen-faced troops at the barricades. These soldiers were not the professionals of peacetime; they were draftees, peasants and workers themselves. Only fear of the punishment they could expect if the revolution failed held them uneasily aloof from the mobs.

By the morning of March 11, police stations throughout Petrograd were in the hands of workers, along with many police weapons and much ammunition. A three-day general strike had been proclaimed by a hastily convened meeting of Menshevik, Bolshevik and Social Revolutionary leaders, to whom the entire uprising had come as a stunning surprise. And, on March 11, the troops had orders to open fire on the mobs. Some obeyed. Sixty workers were shot down by men of the Pavlovsky Regiment. But this incident only aroused angry arguments and fist-fights among the soldiers themselves. That night, in barracks after barracks, the talk waxed hot. The people were making a revolution. To shoot the people meant shooting brothers, sisters, wives. By dawn of March 12, the regiments had decided: the Moscow, the Volynsk, the Litovski, and the Preobrazhensky Regiments shot or imprisoned their officers and came over to the revolution. With bands playing *La Marseillaise*, the soldiers marched through Petrograd, led now by armored cars carrying giant red banners. All Petrograd was in the hands of the revolutionists.

It was so easy, so painfully easy, that many could not believe it. Certainly Nicholas, at his headquarters at the front, did not believe it. When Khabalov telegraphed him for reinforcements on March 10, the Czar replied: "I order that the disorders in the capital be stopped tomorrow." ("I wish it, therefore it must be.") But on March 12, Khabalov was forced to report: "I have at my disposal ...four companies of the Guard, five squadrons of Cos-

A group of revolutionary soldiers firing at one of the Czar's police ambushes in St. Petersburg, February, 1917.

sack cavalry, and two batteries...the rest of the troops have gone over to the revolutionists." Later, puzzling over the rapid evaporation of Czarist power, Khabalov mused about how he had sent regiments forth to crush the revolution. "The regiment starts...under a brave officer, but...there are no results." How could there be "results" when the regiments were composed of draftees, of the very peasants and workers who were supposed to be crushed?

On March 13, Nicholas, at last alarmed, set out in his

A workers' parade where dwarfs masquerade as Rasputin (right) and the hated minister of the interior Protopopov.

private train to rejoin his family in Tsarskoe Selo, outside Petrograd. But the railway workers kept stopping and re-routing the train on an endless and aimless journey all over the countryside. As Trotsky later observed: "With its simple railroad pawns, the revolution had cried 'check' to the king!"

Meanwhile, in Petrograd, all eyes and hopes were fixed on the Tauride Palace. There sat the remnants of the old Duma shaking in their boots and, in another wing of the same building, the new Petrograd Soviet in

Nicholas II in protective custody after his abdication.

which the leaders of all parties of the left, including both Mensheviks and Bolsheviks, joined to establish the new state. N. N. Sukhanov, a Menshevik, described an early meeting of the Soviet: "Standing on stools, their rifles in their hands, agitated and stuttering, straining all their powers to give a concentrated account of the messages that had been given to them...one after another the soldiers' deputies told of what was happening in their companies....The audience listened as children listen to a wonderful, enthralling fairy tale they know by heart... 'we had a meeting...we refuse to serve against the people any more, we're going to join with our brother workers...we would lay down our lives for that!'...storms of applause...."

Delegates were sent to Pskov, where the Czar's train had finally come to rest, to demand his abdication. When a Czarist general took a telephone poll of commanders on the German front, he found that all but one were in mortal fear of their own troops—and they could promise no support for the autocracy. On the night of March 15, Nicholas II signed the document of abdication: "We have thought it good to abdicate from the throne of the Russian State, and to lay down the supreme power....May the Lord God help Russia!" Later, rejoined to his family at Tsarskoe Selo, under "protective custody," Nicholas commented wearily: "There is no justice among men." But generations of untold millions of Russian peasants and workers would not have agreed with him. For the first time since Ivan the Terrible assumed the crown in 1547, there was no Czar in Russia.

THE LONG HOT SUMMER

The basic fact of Russian government in the months following the revolution, was the "dual power." Theoretically, the old Duma, dominated by conservative and liberal middle-class parties, held the power. But the new Petrograd Soviet and its all-powerful Executive Committee, composed of Socialist parties ranging from conservative-minded Mensheviks to implacable Bolsheviks, with the masses of people and the regiments at its command, held the *real* power. The Soviet, feeling it was not yet capable of ruling and dominated by men who believed that a capitalist, middle-class revolution had to be carried out before any Socialist revolution could succeed, needed the Duma and the experienced politicians of the conservative parties. But on the other hand, the Duma's power rested entirely on the continuing support of the Soviet.

Several knotty problems arose immediately, the most important of which was the question of war and peace. The Duma and the Soviet both felt the need of continued Allied support for the "legitimacy" of their rule. There-

The breakdown of "dual power"—Workers stage armed
revolts against the Provisional Government in Petrograd.

fore they were bound to carry on the war, fulfilling Russian obligations under the old Czarist treaties of alliance. But the people, and especially the soldiers, desperately wanted peace—at any price. There was also the question of land reform. If the new Soviet and the Duma did not immediately begin to parcel out the great estates of the aristocracy amongst the poorest peasants, there were signs that the peasants would seize the land anyhow. City workers demanded an eight-hour day, a raise in pay and the dispropriation of the largest factory owners. All—peasants, workers, soldiers—demanded a Constitu-

April 16, 1917. A painting of Lenin greeting welcoming crowds at the Finland Station. Behind him stands the figure of Stalin—this was a later, unhistoric addition.

ent Assembly to draw up a constitution for the new Russian State.

A Soviet dependent on the continuing cooperation of the conservative Duma could meet none of these demands. Instead it temporized and postponed action. Land reform, the workers' demands—all were held in abeyance behind big words. The war continued and a Constituent Assembly was put off to the fall. The masses of people were far to the left of the Soviet, and the subsequent stormy history of the summer of 1917 was but a reflection of the increasing pressure of the people upon their representatives to take immediate revolutionary action.

Meanwhile the Bolshevik exiles, including Lenin in Switzerland and Trotsky in the United States, were trying desperately to return to their homeland. Trotsky, held up by the British who feared his radicalism would further disrupt the vital Russian war effort, was finally permitted to return on the insistence of the new Soviet regime. Lenin, on the other hand, was purposely allowed to pass through Germany in a sealed train, because the German General Staff hoped he would contribute to Russian disruption. By now Lenin had become an all but legendary figure to Russian revolutionists, and especially to his own Bolsheviks. The fact that he, almost alone among Socialist leaders, had steadfastly denounced the war from the beginning, that his writings illuminated and developed the unfinished theses of Marx, that he had selflessly devoted his life to the single end of a Bolshevik triumph—all this lent him tremendous stature in Russian eyes.

Street fighting marked the summer uprisings of 1917.

On April 16, 1917, Lenin arrived at Petrograd's Finland Station. The Bolsheviks had prepared a huge welcome. Thousands jammed the streets leading to the station, huge banners carried Bolshevik slogans, armored cars equipped with searchlights played their beams against the night sky; an honor guard of revolutionary workers and soldiers lined the boulevards. Sukhanov has described Lenin as waiting impatiently through a speech by

the Menshevik President of the Petrograd Soviet, Nicholas Chkeidze, "looking as if all this...did not concern him in the least; he glanced from one side to the other; looked over the surrounding public, and even examined the ceiling." When Chkeidze finished, Lenin spoke. "Dear comrades, soldiers, sailors and workers. I am happy to greet in you the victorious Russian revolution, to greet you as the advance guard of the international proletarian army....The war of imperialist brigandage is the beginning of civil war in Europe....The hour is not far when... the people will turn their arms against their capitalist exploiters....Long live the International Social Revolution!"

"Suddenly," Sukhanov related, "before the eyes of all of us, completely swallowed up by the routine drudgery of the revolution, there was presented a bright, blinding, exotic light." The light became clearer when Lenin harangued his party comrades later at a private meeting. "We don't need any parliamentary republic," he thundered; "we don't need any bourgeois democracy. We don't need any government except the Soviet of Workers', Soldiers', and Peasants' Deputies!" From that moment, the Bolshevik Party dedicated itself to forcing all state power onto the Soviet and seizing control of the Soviet itself.

The figure behind which the Mensheviks and conservative Socialists of the Soviet gathered in these days was Alexander Kerensky, a brilliant but wordy and weak-willed lawyer who was the only Socialist in the Provisional Government selected from the Duma. An ambitious man, Kerensky was given to compromise, plotting and hysterics. Sukhanov relates how one day, when shots were heard outside the Tauride Palace, "Kerensky rushed to the window, leaped on the sill, and sticking his head out shouted in a hoarse, broken voice: 'Stations everyone! Defend the Duma! Listen to me—I, Kerensky, am speaking to you....' It was clear that the shots were accidental....'Everything's all right,' I said in a low voice ...Kerensky broke into a rage and began bellowing...

'I demand—that everyone—do his duty—and not interfere —when I—give orders!' "

In April, following a public promise by the Provisional Government that it would abide by the Czarist treaties and carry on the war, masses of people demonstrated through the streets of Petrograd. A witness of this event wrote: "About a hundred armed men marched in front; after them solid phalanxes of unarmed men and women, a thousand strong...Songs...Their faces amazed me. All those thousands had but one face, the stunned ecstatic face of the early Christian monks. Implacable, pitiless..." The demonstrations forced the Soviet to take more power in the Provisional Government, and to disavow certain agreements with the Allies.

In June, the Socialist parties held rival demonstrations in Mars Field, in Petrograd. To the horror of the Mensheviks and conservative Socialists, Bolshevik slogans, banners and phalanxes completely dominated the gathering. It was in June, also, that Kerensky and the Provisional Government launched a new offensive against the Germans. Under pressure from the Allies, they felt they had no choice. By July 16, the Russian Armies had predictably completely broken down and were again in headlong retreat.

The disasters of the July offensive, combined with continuing procrastination over reforms on the home front, produced a spontaneous attempt by the Petrograd workers to seize power from the Duma and from a Soviet they felt had betrayed them. But they acted without effective leadership (the Bolsheviks were against the uprising) and

"Worker Ivanov"—Lenin disguised for escape to Finland.

A meeting of the Provisional Government in April, 1917.

suffered a bloody defeat at the hands of regiments loyal to the Provisional Government. Seizing on the occasion, Kerensky and the Soviet joined Duma leaders in accusing Lenin and the Bolsheviks of having brought on the uprising as part of a German plot to ruin the Russian war effort. Forged papers were circulated which tried to prove that Lenin, Trotsky and other Bolshevik leaders were agents of Imperial Germany. While Lenin escaped to Finland, Trotsky and other Bolsheviks were imprisoned in the old Peter and Paul Czarist fortress in Petrograd. Moreover, most Russians seemed willing to believe the charges against the Bolsheviks. By the end of July, 1917, it appeared that the new Russian government, with Kerensky as Prime Minister, was firmly in control of the country and that the Bolsheviks had at last been effectively eliminated.

THE OCTOBER REVOLUTION

f there were any lesson to be learned from observation of events in Russia it was that appearances were often deceiving. Nor was the government threatened only from the left. For now the rightist reactionaries were also prepared to strike their blow. Hero and leader of the re-emboldened rightists was Lavr Georgievich Kornilov, son of a Siberian Cossack, sometime Army commander on the Austrian front and now Kerensky's Commander-in-Chief of all Russian armies. The liberal politician and historian Paul Milyukov described Kornilov as a "short, stumpy but strong figure of a man with Kalmuck features...darting sharp piercing glances from his small black eyes in which there was a vicious glint."

While Kerensky hoped to use Kornilov to destroy the Petrograd Soviet, Kornilov hoped not only to destroy the Soviet but also Kerensky and all the other hated apparatus of parliamentary government. And as the two men laid their plots, Socialists of all parties grew alarmed at the prospect of a Czarist restoration. The Petrograd Soviet secretly organized a military committee for the

Alexander Kerensky, head of the Provisional Government.

General Lavr Kornilov, leader of the reactionary forces.

defense of the revolution which included many Bolsheviks, who had recovered their prestige from the July
days. Volunteer Red Guard companies and battalions
were armed by the Soviet from government arsenals.

Early in September, Kornilov made his move. Several
divisions of "trustworthy" troops, which had been pulled
away from the front, were ordered to march on Petrograd. The workers prepared to defend themselves. But
as Kornilov's divisions advanced they were met by agitators sent out by the Soviet. "Almost everywhere," reported one of Kornilov's generals sadly, "we saw one
and the same picture. On the tracks or in the [railway]

cars, or in the saddles of their black or bay horses...
dragoons would be sitting or standing, and in the midst
of them some lively personality in a soldier's long coat."
That lively personality was the revolution's secret
weapon—a man able to explain to the troops just what
Kornilov intended them to do, what it would mean to
them to crush the revolution. Like magic, Kornilov's
soldiers simply melted away before Petrograd, while in
Moscow and Kiev gigantic demonstrations were held
against him. Kornilov's generals were arrested by their
own men, some were hanged, some shot, and some were
made prisoner, like Kornilov himself.

The Kornilov revolt gave powerful impetus to Bolshe-
vism throughout Russia. It was apparent that Kerensky
had been intriguing with the general. Now all the Bolshevik predictions and maledictions seemed to be coming
true. Trotsky and other Bolshevik leaders were released
from prison, although Lenin continued in his Finnish
exile. By the end of September the Bolsheviks had won
majorities in elections to the Executive Committees of the
Moscow, Kiev and Petrograd Soviets. The Bolshevik
slogan had been "All Power to the Soviets!" Now they
were the Soviets. Only Kerensky and his ghostly Duma-
supported government stood between them and absolute
power.

On September 25, Lenin, writing from Finland, urged
the Bolsheviks to carry out an armed insurrection. He
pointed out that peasants throughout Russia were burn-
ing manor-houses, seizing the land and killing any un-
fortunate landlords who fell into their hands; that city

workers were flocking to the Bolshevik banners; that the Army had shown it would back the Bolshevik program once it was explained to them.

Trotsky, the energetic man-on-the-spot, was placed in charge of preparations and given over-all command of the insurrection. He worked with demonic energy to arm the workers' Red Guard, laying precise and careful plans. On October 23, Lenin returned secretly from Finland disguised in a wig. On November 4, the Petrograd Soviet held large meetings of workers within their respective factories, at which Bolshevik orators harangued them. On November 5, Kerensky, now thoroughly alarmed, declared that an emergency existed and placed Petrograd under martial law. But most people in Petrograd no longer paid any attention to Kerensky or his government. Instead they flocked for orders to Bolshevik headquarters at the Smolny Institute. American reporter John Reed was there to see. "The long, vaulted corridors, lit by rare electric lights, were thronged with hurrying shapes of soldiers and workmen, some bent under the weight of huge bundles of newspapers, proclamations, printed propaganda of all sorts. The sound of their heavy boots made a deep and incessant thunder on the wooden floor." Beneath that thunder, the old Russia was disappearing forever.

On the night of November 6, the Bolsheviks struck. Police stations, railway stations, communications centers, government offices, banks, factories and businesses were taken over or placed under guard by workers' militia. On the morning of November 7 all Petrograd, with

The weakly-defended Winter Palace fell in five hours.

the exception of the Winter Palace in which some members of the defunct Kerensky regime were holed up, was in Bolshevik hands. Kerensky himself had escaped, disguised beneath a woman's shawl in an American Embassy car. The Winter Palace was surrounded by Bolshevik troops and defended only by raw cadets and a women's volunteer battalion. At 9 P.M. the Bolshevik crew of the cruiser *Aurora*, anchored in the Neva opposite the Palace, opened fire; so did Bolshevik gunners in the nearby fortress of Peter and Paul. By 2 A.M. on the morning of November 8, it was over. The Kerensky government was in prison or hiding, the Bolsheviks were triumphant, and

Trotsky (left) and Lenin harangue the Petrograd workers.

almost no blood had been shed.

Shortly after the fall of the Winter Palace, Lenin appeared in public for the first time since his escape to Finland to address a riotous meeting of the All-Russian Congress of Soviets. Some Menshevik delegates walked out. But most stayed to cheer. John Reed reported: "Now Lenin, gripping the edge of the reading stand, let little winking eyes travel over the crowd as he stood there waiting, apparently oblivious to the long-rolling ovation. ...When it finished he said simply, 'We shall now proceed to construct the socialist order.' Again that overwhelming human roar."

THE CIVIL WAR

The Bolshevik victory was not everywhere as bloodless as it had been in Petrograd. There was bitter fighting in Moscow and in Kiev, Ukrainian separatists seized the occasion to set up a separate Ukrainian government. Similar separatist groups seized power in certain areas of Siberia and the Caucasus. Kerensky had fled to the front to raise regiments against Bolshevik Petrograd, but Trotsky followed him and found, to his relief, that Kerensky's appeals had failed.

The first order of business for the Bolshevik government was the inescapable necessity of concluding a speedy peace with Germany. On December 3, 1917, a Soviet delegation arrived at the city of Brest-Litovsk to open negotiations with representatives of the German General Staff. The Germans, faced with the arrival of a flood of American divisions on the Western Front, were now almost as eager as the Russians for peace in the East. But Trotsky (in charge of the negotiations) still hoped for Allied support of the new government and de-

World War I deserters returning to their Russian homes.

layed the negotiations until the Germans simply began to advance again. On March 3, 1918, Russia left the war. By the infamous treaty of Brest-Litovsk she lost one-third of her population and one-quarter of her territory to Germany.

The collapse of Russia was a disaster to the Allied cause. Allied commanders worried about the huge supplies of guns and munitions stockpiled at Archangel and Vladivostok: there seemed nothing to prevent the Germans from simply seizing them. And, more importantly,

February, 1918. The Russian delegation led by Trotsky (center) is greeted by the Germans at Brest-Litovsk.

Allied governments and ruling circles viewed the Bolsheviks with horror and fear. England, France and Japan determined to intervene in Russia with men and supplies. The United States, although determined *not* to intervene, was dragged into various expeditions through a combination of poor intelligence and Allied swindling. Thus American troops accompanied the British on a comic-opera intervention at Archangel which ended ingloriously, and joined the Japanese at Vladivostok (more to keep them from seizing Siberia than to put down the

The famed Cossack cavalry during a Civil War battle.

Food shortages became acute in 1918. Detachments were sent into the countryside to scour for supplies (top), and soup kitchens for children were set up in Petrograd.

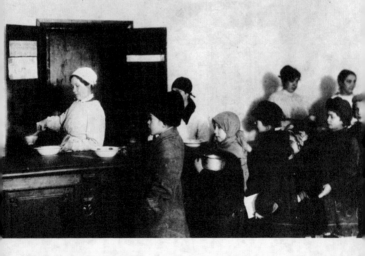

But wartime starvation continued to claim many victims.

Red Army generals Kalinin and Budenny muster forces.

Allied officers gather with the Japanese at Vladivostok following their ill-advised intervention at Archangel.

Bolsheviks).

Behind the hopes entertained for Allied intervention, was the growing chaos in Russia and the opening of civil war. Various Russian generals of the old regime were organizing followers in different sections of the country. General Denikin in the Ukraine, Admiral Kolchak and General Kornilov in Siberia, General Kaledin, leader of the Don Cossacks — all now raised the banner of rebellion, and all received support in varying degree from Allied forces in Russia.

Another element of chaos was the Czech Legion, a well-armed, well-trained body of men who had deserted from the Austrian army and been formed in Russia to fight their way back to what they hoped would be an independent Czech nation. These men marched, fought and looted their way across Siberia, seizing most of the Trans-Siberian Railroad in the process, towards Vladivostok where Allied ships waited to carry them to the Western

A ragged group of Russian Communist infiltrators taken by strong counter-revolutionary forces in the Ukraine.

Front. But on their heroic journey they joined forces with various Russian rebels to fight the Bolsheviks. It was the approach of the Czech Legion that brought about the death of the former Royal Family. Nicholas, Alix and their children were being held in the town of Ekaterinburg in the Ural mountains. Local Bolshevik authorities, fearing the oncoming Czechs would free Nicholas, who would then become the center of anti-Bolshevik resistance, shot and bayoneted the entire family on July 16, 1918. The murderers were later executed by Lenin's government.

The disruption of the civil war also brought opportunity to various national groups who had long dreamt of breaking out of the "Prison of Nations." The Finns, the people of the little Baltic States—Latvia, Esthonia and Lithuania—and the Poles all established their independence during 1918-1919. Soviet armies had to cope with civil war on a dozen fronts, Allied armies of intervention, and national-liberation armies in the west. Yet gradually they won—the civil war, at least. The Bolshevik hero of those chaotic years was undoubtedly Trotsky. Rushing from front to front in an armored train, haranguing and inspiring the troops, plotting strategy for the new Red Armies and making deals with local populations, he revealed himself as a brilliant military tactician as well as politician.

But the basic reason for the collapse of the various rebellions was simply that, being inspired by reactionary leaders, they quickly lost the support of the people wherever they established their regimes. Most of their men

The royal family in custody tastes the workers' life.
Top, Anastasia with Bolshevik guards a few days before
her death. Bottom, Olga, Alexis, Anastasia and Tatiana.

War Commissar Leon Trotsky, the mastermind behind the Red Army throughout the years of Civil War in Russia.

revealed themselves as savage freebooters intent primarily on rape, murder and looting. In the Ukraine, the approach of anti-Bolshevik forces was generally heralded by anti-Jewish pogroms and massacres. And if the rebel forces could win no popular support, they soon lost the military support of the Allies. The people of the Allied nations were utterly war-weary after the terrible bloodletting of the Great War, and their governments were soon forced to withdraw their troops. By 1920 the last foreign soldiers had left Russian soil.

The Paris Peace Conference of 1919, from which Soviet representatives were excluded, stripped Russia of Poland, Latvia, Esthonia, Lithuania, Finland and parts of the Ukraine. But Lenin and the Bolsheviks considered themselves well out of it. The Red Army had grown into an efficient military machine (it almost captured Warsaw in 1920 but was driven back by the Poles under French leadership and with French supplies), and the Soviets were now free to deploy it against domestic enemies. One by one, Admiral Kolchak in Siberia, General Denikin in the Ukraine, Generals Wrangel and Kornilov were forced back, captured, killed or driven into exile. The Czechs were sent home.

Something of the horror, tragedy and chaos of the civil war was observed by Russian writer Konstantin Paustovsky, as he watched Denikin's followers flee from Odessa when the Red Army approached. Crowding down to the waterfront, huge throngs struggled to board the few boats in the harbor. "People literally destroyed each other, not letting even those save themselves who could

A cavalry of Russian workers and peasants rides forth to fight for the Bolshevik government in the Civil War.

A bearded peasant pleads for the Communist cause with his neighbors beneath a wreathed portrait of Lenin.

Russian refugees, who are trying to flee from the new Communist state, bed down for the night in a train depot.

The Bolshevik victory is complete. Across the continent in Vladivostok a parade for the new Communist leaders.

anage to crawl up the gangways and grab the railing
a ship. Several arms would reach out at once to
utch the lucky man and to hang onto him. He would
ch forward, along the gangway, dragging the other
gitives behind him, until the gangway itself collapsed
nd dropped him into the sea to drown.... All the roads
ading to the port were jammed with people." Hundreds
ere trampled to death in the melee. Then the boats
ulled away, listing terribly under their human loads.
From the city one could hear, faintly, the singing of a
tanza of the 'Internationale.' "

SOCIALISM
VERSUS
STALINISM

A QUESTION OF TACTICS

The Bolshevik victory belonged to many people, but especially to Lenin and Trotsky. As Edmund Wilson observes, these men had fitted and adapted, for the first time in human history, a theoretical-philosophical key (Marxism) to a real historical lock. They had made a revolution and won a civil war; now they had to build a state. But the creation of a new government, a new economy, a new consciousness among Russia's almost illiterate millions—these were problems for which there were no theoretical guides. Something of the spirit with which the Bolsheviks approached their task was revealed in an editorial in the Party newspaper *Pravda* (Truth) which appeared just after the October Revolution: "They wanted us to take the power alone, so that we alone should have to contend with the terrible difficulties confronting the country.... So be it!...They dreamed of a dictatorship of Kornilov. ...We will give them the dictatorship of the proletariat!"

The difficulties were indeed terrible. Lenin and his followers had inherited a country whose essential primi-

A vote for Stalin, while Comrade Molotov waits his turn.

Lenin and his wife Nadezhda Krupskaya in their garden at Gorki with their nephews, shortly before Lenin's death.

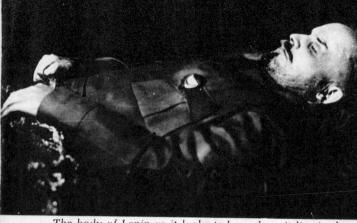

The body of Lenin as it looks today, where it lies in the marble mausoleum on Red Square in the Moscow Kremlin.

tiveness was now compounded by years of war and devastation. Industry was at a standstill, the transportation system wrecked, the national currency was worthless and huge areas of the best agricultural land had been taken out of production by peasants for fear that their land would be confiscated. Furthermore the Communists, as they now dubbed themselves officially, were handicapped by vast administrative inexperience and by continuing opposition from many quarters. In their seizure of power they had cooperated with militant elements among the Social Revolutionary Party which represented millions of Russian peasants. But during the months of civil war, the Social Revolutionaries found themselves quickly and ruthlessly driven from government. Early in 1918, Fanya Kaplan, a young SR disillusioned by Communist tactics, attempted to kill Lenin, and succeeded in lodging two bullets in his neck and shoulder. Lenin recovered, but Communist vengeance was terrible. Prisons already full of monarchists and reactionaries were now crammed with Social Revolutionaries, Mensheviks and other non-Communist leftists. The dreaded *Cheka* ("Extraordinary Commission"), created originally as a weapon against Czarist conspirators, was now loosed against all opponents of the new regime, no matter what their political convictions. The *Cheka* soon proved itself far more efficient and brutal than the old Czarist secret police. Over the years it changed its name (it was to become the GPU and, later, the NKVD) but never its methods.

But while activist opponents could be murdered or imprisoned by the *Cheka,* Russia's real economic problems could not be simply decreed away. Primary among these was the complete breakdown of food production and distribution. The revolution had given the peasants the land they had so long coveted. But now they were told that although they occupied the land, everything they grew upon it (with the exception of what they were allowed for subsistence) had to be turned over to the government. Under these circumstances, the peasants simply refused to grow more food than they needed. Punitive expeditions of Army units sent out from Moscow might bring terror to the countryside, but they could produce no food. Droughts, the ravages of war, and the breakdown of communications completed the agricultural debacle. By 1921 Russia was in the grip of a desperate famine. American food relief (administered by the Quakers) could alleviate but not solve the problem. Furthermore, with industry all but dead and the currency so valueless that it required 100,000 rubles to purchase a loaf of bread in Moscow in 1921, complete economic disaster stared the new government in the face.

Lenin, always more pragmatic than doctrinaire, determined on a new and bold departure from Communist dogma to solve these problems. In March, 1921, the Communists announced the New Economic Policy (NEP) which established a mixed economy. Transportation, large industry such as steel mills, mines and other raw material sources, and foreign trade were all to remain government-owned monopolies. But small businesses were free to operate as capitalistic free enterprises, and the peasants were permitted to sell a large share of their produce on the open market. Under the NEP, the Russian economy slowly but steadily recovered. Food production began to ease the famines of 1921-1923, industry was reorganized and, by 1924 even surpassed its highest Czarist levels of production.

In that same year, however, the Communists suffered a blow from which they were not to recover for generations—the death of Vladimir Lenin. Having never really recovered from Fanya Kaplan's bullet, in May, 1922 he suffered a stroke, which was followed by another in December, 1922, and a third in March, 1923. On January 21, 1924, the founder of the new Russian state succumbed to a final, fatal stroke. Of his passing, Winston Churchill observed: "He alone could have found the way back to the causeway.... The Russian people were left floundering in the bog. Their worst misfortune was his birth... their next worse, his death." He was given a tremendous state funeral and Petrograd, the city of Peter, was, appropriately, renamed Leningrad, the city of Lenin. Yet even before his death the struggle for his power had begun.

Lenin's heirs — Stalin, Kamenev, Tomsky, Kalinin, Bukharin, Molotov and Zinoviev — carry his funeral bier, while hundreds of mourners march along the Moscow streets.

DESTRUCTION OF A DREAM

Lenin, Trotsky and their followers had always understood that Marxian communism, which depended for its successful application on a highly industrialized state, could not be built on the backward peasant economy of Russia. But they had believed that the Russian revolution would spark similar revolutions throughout Europe and thus bring them the vital support of advanced industrial nations such as Germany and France. In western Europe, however, Communist uprisings had been put down wherever they had occurred — especially in Hungary and Germany. By 1924 it was becoming clear to the more practical Communist leaders that a world-wide or even continent-wide revolution was not going to take place. Furthermore, the administrators and functionaries of the Party were by nature, aptitude and necessity much more concerned about the daily practical problems of ruling their own country than about the fortunes of the struggling Chinese or Spanish Communist Parties. Although they were not theorists, the Communist "practicals" developed a theory of "building

Leon Trotsky gives a speech in Copenhagen after he has been ousted by Stalin and exiled from the Soviet Union.

Socialism in one country." This concept was blasphemy to those Communist leaders like Trotsky, who had made the revolution. But in the years between 1917 and 1924 the "practicals" had gained tremendous power both in the state and in the Party—in the manner of all bureaucracies.

One of the most practical of the "practicals" was Joseph Vissarionovich Dzhugashvili, a short, powerfully-built man who came from Russian Georgia and spoke Russian with the accent of his primitive and but recently-Russianized mountaineer forebears. Born in 1879, Dzhugashvili, the son of a small-town cobbler, studied for the Russian Orthodox priesthood as a young man. But his superiors at the seminary in Tiflis, discovering he studied Plekhanov's translation of Marx with more relish than the lives of the saints, had him expelled. In 1899 he joined the Bolsheviks and, after meeting Lenin in Switzerland, was assigned to very practical work indeed—the wheedling and stealing of money to finance Party activities. Young Dzhugashvili showed great aptitude as a bandit, and also as a double agent. For years he served the Czarist secret police as an informer, all the while carrying on his Party work. He was arrested seven times before 1913, and in that year was sent into Siberian exile. Returning to Petrograd under the amnesty proclaimed by the first Revolutionary government in 1917, he was appointed editor of the Bolshevik newspaper, *Pravda*. During the long hot summer of Bolshevik maneuvering for power, he could be counted on to either support the conservative view or keep his mouth shut at Party conferences. He was adept at waiting to see which way the

Party majority would go, and then proclaiming the new policies as if they were his own. The truth was that Dzhugashvili, though ruthless and intelligent, was not an intellectual. Indeed, he was profoundly ill-at-ease in that rarefied theoretical atmosphere through which Lenin and Trotsky moved so easily. Also, as his early career had indicated, he was ravenous for personal power. Because of his foreign background, Lenin had appointed him Commissar of Nationalities in the new government. In 1922 he won the post of general secretary of the Communist Party, at which point his own ruthless practicality met and fused with the uninspired practicality of the vast governing bureaucracy. But by that time he was no longer known as Dzhugashvili, but by his old conspiratorial name Stalin, "made of steel."

In his struggle for power with Trotsky and the internationalist heirs of Lenin, Stalin used the concept of socialism in one country as his chief weapon. The Party bureaucracy, which of necessity had grown up within the shell of Leninist intellectual leadership, cracked out of that shell on Lenin's death, and took control. Trotsky and his followers were voted down at Party Congresses, and Trotsky himself was demoted, then exiled to Siberia and, finally, in 1929 exiled from Russia. He wandered the world preaching his international Socialist revolution, correctly interpreting and forecasting the deepening Stalinist tyranny which overtook his homeland, and terrifying Stalin as only an activist intellectual *could* terrify an essentially plodding administrator. In 1940 Stalin's vengeance overtook him in Mexico and he was axed to death by a Communist assassin.

At the Fifteenth Party Congress held in December, 1927, Stalin unveiled his plans for building socialism in Russia: broadly encompassed within the first Five Year Plan his plans aimed at a massive and forced collectivization of the land, and the establishment of a powerful industrial plant. Worked out in great detail by laboring bureaucrats, the Five Year Plan was the first attempt in human history to organize precisely the economic structure and future growth of a national state. It established the basic matrix of Russian society for years to come— and it spelled the death of the Marxist-Leninist dream of world proletarian brotherhood.

One of the numerous Russian churches that Stalin had wrecked to supply materials for "useful" constructions.

Joseph Stalin, dictator of Russia, photographed in 1928.

TRANSFORMATION OF A NATION

The several Five Year Plans which ran concurrently, sometimes overlapping, got under way in 1928. There were good years when production quotas were met, and there were bad years when this or that aspect of one of the plans fell behind. But all the years were *forced* ones as Russia under Stalin became a great forcing-house of industrialization, collectivization and centralization. Russia, which meant the Russian people, was directed to establish, within a decade or two, one of the world's great industrial empires. What had been accomplished in the United States, Germany and other capitalist nations over a period of a century was to be accomplished under socialism within twenty years. This goal was not met. But that it was even approached was little less than miraculous.

The first Five Year Plan (1928-1933) brought into existence over one hundred entirely new industrial cities. Ambitious projects such as the Dniepropetrovsk dam in the Ukraine and the Volga-Don canal were begun, often with the assistance of American and English engineers who had come to Russia with the relaxation of anti-Western

The Five Year Plans—A Red Army soldier teaches two
peasants in Uzbek how to operate a "modern" tractor.

suspicion under Lenin's NEP. Steel mills suddenly started belching smoke into distant Siberian skies; agricultural regions sprouted with "tractor stations"; mines and the vast oil resources of the Caucasus were re-equipped, their output rationalized; and the vital machine-tool industry increased production many times over. The second Five Year Plan made some concessions to consumer needs. The streets of towns and provincial cities and even certain sections of Leningrad and Moscow received their first coats of asphalt and their first Soviet-built cars. Sir Bernard Pares observed: "In 1931 there were hardly any cars; by 1935 I found the streets covered with them. Naturally...a levelling down went with the levelling up. Good boots were rare, but the unshod now had mediocre footwear." Mediocre was perhaps a kind word to apply to many Soviet products. Often in the hands of dogmatic and totally inexperienced bureaucratic managers, the new machinery was damaged daily by incompetent workmen. But Russians had only to compare their standard of living during the thirties with that of the past to be eminently satisfied.

From the beginning the Communists were painfully aware of their desperate need for skilled technicians and scientists. And their earliest and most successful efforts went into creating a new educational system. Schools by the thousands were opened throughout the country and within two decades the Russian illiteracy rate had fallen from over 75% to less than 5%. What the students read was another matter. The schools were fountainheads of Marxist doctrine and Communist propaganda and the strictest control was exercised over both teachers and curricula. But on the higher educational levels Marxist dogma had to give way to practical expediency. If the Communist student devoted himself exclusively to Marxist theory he would undoubtedly fail in his subject; but if he devoted himself solely to a study of his subject he might well be led away from Communist belief. The problem of producing highly skilled technicians, one half of whose brains were to be devoted to the search for abstract truth and competence in increasingly complicated disciplines while the other half of their brains were supposed to wallow in fanatical adherence to outdated doctrines, was one which the Communists were never to solve.

Difficult as it was to industrialize agricultural Russia, it was infinitely more difficult to socialize Russian agriculture. Stalin had determined to introduce widespread collectivization of farming as an essential complement to industrialization. But in order to accomplish this it would be necessary to wage an all-out political war against the peasant proprietors of the land. Since the Revolution, and especially since the NEP, the Russian peasantry had steadily been developing "classes"—that is, the shrewder or richer peasants had increased their holdings while a larger and larger proportion of peasants had become farm laborers. Stalin assumed that the farm laboring class would welcome collectivization as a rescue from exploitation by their more fortunate neighbors. Therefore in 1928 collectivization was begun under the banners of a crusade against the *Kulaks* (the word means "fist"), the rich peasants. By decree the Kulaks overnight found themselves stripped of their land, their houses, and often even of their liberty, as hundreds of thousands were shipped to labor camps. Military expeditions backed up Moscow's directives and a plague of Party bureaucrats descended on the Russian land to carry out Stalin's policy.

But the city theoreticians found their programs bitterly opposed by rich and poor peasants alike. Maurice Hindus, who visited many a Russian village during the war against the Kulaks, reported an old peasant blacksmith telling him: "There was a time...when we were just neighbors in the village. We quarreled, we fooled, sometimes we cheated one another, but we were neighbors. Now we are poor, middle and Kulaks...and we are supposed to have a class war.... What the Devil!"

Faced with the choice of either voluntarily entering collective farms, or being classified as Kulaks and deported to slave-labor camps in Siberia, the peasants struck back in the only way they knew. Rather than turn over their tools, houses and livestock to the government, they destroyed them. Crops were burned in the fields; more than 17,000,000 horses were killed, 30,000,000 head of cattle and nearly 100,000,000 sheep and goats. Entire villages declared themselves autonomous and had to be subdued in pitched battles by Red Army units. The small-scale civil war which raged over the Russian land during the early thirties naturally produced famine. But since it was the peasants who were resisting the government, the authorities saw to it that this time it was the peasants who starved, not the city people. Starvation became an

State home and school for workers' children in the '30's.

Construction of a coke-chemical plant in the South Urals.

Peasants line up to register for work on collective farms.

effective weapon against the peasants—so effective that
estimates of peasant deaths brought on by famine, execu-
tion and deportation from 1929 to 1933 range from eight
to ten million! In the end, of course, the state won. The
peasants went into the collective farms and were organized into "brigades" to mow, reap, sow and harvest. The
government bought (at prices far below market value) all
the production of the collective, except what was needed
by the collective's members for their own consumption.
Sir John Maynard, the English agricultural expert, esti-

mated that in 1936 the average peasant's earnings were
still less than they had been before the Revolution. But on
the other hand, the cultivated area had increased by 25%.

In embarking on his Five Year Plans, Stalin had determined to impose socialism on a country unprepared for
it, according to Socialist theory itself. His success in
creating a tremendous industrial complex and collec-
tivizing the land would seem to have proved Socialist
theory wrong. But that theory had never foreseen absolute dictatorship and genocide as its paths to success.

THE GREAT PURGES

If Lenin had identified himself with history, and Trotsky history with himself, Stalin did neither. Instead he identified himself with the state until he became the state. And in this dictator's progressively deranged mind, all who disagreed with him became "traitors," "wreckers," or "saboteurs," to be dealt with as dangerous enemies of the state. Stalin's entire life and career may be viewed as the deepening obsession of a paranoid personality to retain "control," at ever more desperate cost, of his nightmarish environment. Whoever threatened him—intellectuals, artists, political opponents, inefficient managers who botched production, foreign governments, doctors, peasants—all were marked for eventual liquidation. But Stalin was also shrewd. Not for him the stupid, open-handed repression of the Czars which had only succeeded in uniting the masses against the state. His "control," his personal vengeances and his nation-wide repressions were all to be artfully contrived to *divide* possible opposition, were to be masked behind progressive slogans, patriotic fanfares and sober Marxist

The Purges—Stalin heads up the funeral procession of
V. Menzhinsky, former chief of the secret police, who
reportedly died of a strange "paralysis of the heart."

incantations.

The Bolsheviks, on the crest of enthusiasm with which they had overthrown the old political order, had sought also to decree a new interpersonal order into Russian life. Religion, viewed by Marxists as one of their most dangerous enemies, had been all but stamped out. Convents and monasteries were emptied, the churches and cathedrals were turned into museums, and an anti-religious propaganda barrage, aimed especially at the young, was effectively launched. Marriage, seen as simply another "bourgeois" institution, was also derided. Free love, temporary alliances and easy divorce had been the order of the day before Stalin's take-over. Progressive theories of education (especially those of the American

philosopher John Dewey) had been eagerly tried. Avant-garde experiments in the arts had been encouraged. Poets such as Mayakovsky, Blok and Pasternak, musicians such as the young Prokofiev and Shostakovitch, had been applauded and had produced some strikingly original work. But all this changed after 1929. To Stalin's puritanical background experiments in sex-relationships, education, and the arts were "degenerate." Besides, he did not understand them; therefore they were dangerous. In the schools rigid discipline was reintroduced after 1934; in the law courts it was made all but impossible to obtain a divorce; artists who could not produce in the new style of "Socialist Realism" (a banal, photographic fidelity to reality, choosing for topics either Stalin him-

Vyshinsky's speech justifying the purge trials of the "Trotskyites" is read aloud in every Russian factory.

self, or "heroic" scenes of workers or peasants happily over-fulfilling production norms) were suppressed. In 1930 the poet Mayakovsky committed suicide, and with his death a profound silence settled over Soviet literature.

In 1935 commenced that fantastic nightmare in Russian history which was to become known as the "Great Purge." There were actually a whole series of purges, ornamented now and then by show trials and carried out by the NKVD. The object was to liquidate any and all opposition to the Stalinist regime. But since the possibility of opposition was defined only by the suspicions of Stalin's paranoid mentality, the liquidations became a gigantic program of mass imprisonment and murder. The purge completely wiped out the entire corps of Old Bolsheviks (even Lenin's closest associates); then went on to destroy all former opponents such as Mensheviks, anarchists, Social Revolutionaries. It claimed the lives of individuals displaying religious affiliation, those who had been abroad and might therefore have become "contaminated," foreign Communists who had sought refuge in Russia, Communist Party members who opposed the purges, anyone who had ever made a mistake in administration and production; and finally—the armed forces. Estimates of the number of victims of the Great Purge range from eight million to twenty million.

The theory under which the purge was carried out, and which illuminated the Moscow Trials of 1936-1938, was that Russia was menaced by a conspiracy which embraced capitalist nations, a huge Russian underground and, above all, Trotskyites both at home and abroad.

Stalin blamed this conspiracy for the clumsiness and brutalities of the Five Year Plans, for the famines, the production failures, the poor harvests and even earthquakes. At carefully rehearsed public trials, one after another, the former commissars, Party leaders, field marshals and generals arose to make abject confessions of having plotted with Hitler or the Mikado or J. P. Morgan (all through the cunning agency of Trotsky) to wreck plants, poison fields, lead rebellions, sell state secrets and murder government officials. The rest of the world, represented at the "open" trials in Moscow by hundreds of newspapermen, looked on aghast and bewildered as the biggest names in Soviet officialdom declared themselves "wreckers," "saboteurs" and "running dogs of foreign imperialism." The charges brought against these victims were so obviously ridiculous, their fate (death) so apparently predetermined that outsiders could not understand why they degraded themselves with futile confessions, why some at least did not seize the opportunity to expose the Stalinist terror for what it was. But this was not the psychology of the revolutionist. These men who were now being devoured by their revolution had devoted their entire lives to it. They were doomed in any case. To conclude that they were personally guilty of mistakes, even of crimes, was perhaps easier than to admit to themselves that the object of their existence, the revolution which had given their lives meaning, was itself at fault. Besides, the NKVD had ways and means of brutalizing and breaking the spirit of those who refused to cooperate—one of the most effective being the

Lev Kamenev on the stand at his purge trial in 1936.

promise that their families might be spared if they sacrificed themselves. So Grinko, former Secretary of the Treasury, said: "I knew and was connected with people ...in the Red Army who were preparing to open the frontier to the enemy." Krestinsky, former Undersecretary of State, said: "We came to an agreement with General Seekt [Chief of the German General Staff]...we would help the Reichswehr create a number of espionage bases in the territory of the USSR....In return for this the Reichswehr undertook to pay us 250,000 marks annually...."

The damage done by the Great Purge to Russian production was tremendous. Technicians especially felt the hand of the NKVD; knowledge, even technical knowl-

Dictator Stalin again at one of his common pastimes.

edge, was suspect in itself. But the chaos created in Russian industry was as nothing compared to the catastrophe which overwhelmed the Red Army command structure. Three out of five field marshals, thirteen out of fifteen army generals and 65% of all other officers, down to and including the rank of colonel, were liquidated. Had the "running dogs of foreign imperialism" really planned a blow against the Soviet Union they could hardly have wreaked more damage than did Stalin's mad Great Purge. But that was merely the view from outside the Soviet Union. From within the Kremlin walls, after 1938, Stalin and his followers could look out over a nation completely and totally within their grasp. All opposition had perished.

THE STEADY DRUMMER

But beyond the ramparts of the Kremlin also lay a hostile world, one which Lenin had predicted would one day turn to strike at the bastion of socialism. The hopes of Communist revolutions in other lands had gone a-glimmering during the twenties. The German Communists, organized into the Spartakist League, had attempted to seize power in 1919, only to be crushed by an alliance of Social Democratic politicians and the German army. Karl Liebknecht and Rosa Luxemburg, Spartakist leaders and close friends of Lenin, had been brutally murdered in Berlin. The temporary success in 1919 of Bela Kun's Communist rising in Hungary raised Bolshevik hopes for a moment, but this rebellion was also speedily crushed. Yet Lenin's and Trotsky's insistence on the necessity for Communist successes in western Europe, as a safeguard for the Communist take-over in Russia, was not entirely without foundation. The fact of Communist rebellions, and the upsurge of strength shown by such non-Communist left groups as the British Labor Party, un-

The Communist Party outside of the Soviet Union. 1930
May Day Parade around Union Square in New York City.

doubtedly stayed the hands of those western European leaders who might have been tempted to intervene massively in the new Soviet Union.

Lenin had seen clearly that one way to keep capitalist nations too busy to attack Russia was to foment trouble in their colonies. At world-wide gatherings of Socialist leaders in Moscow he hammered home the thesis of turning national-liberation wars into Communist-directed anti-Western struggles. And of all the wars of national liberation during the twenties, the struggle of the Chinese people to unify themselves and throw off the domination of English, French, American and Japanese imperialisms seemed the most promising. Russian advisors and supplies were accordingly dispatched to Sun Yat Sen's Kuomintang Party as early as 1922. And the infant Chinese Communist Party was instructed to cooperate with the Kuomintang in every respect—over the objections of one of the Party's minor members, Mao Tse-tung.

After Lenin's death, Stalin did not alter this policy of all-out support for the Kuomintang. When Sun Yat Sen died in 1925, and control of the Kuomintang passed to the young General Chiang Kai-shek, Moscow was well satisfied. Chiang had studied military tactics in Soviet Russia and expressed himself as "impressed" by Soviet achievements. In spite of warnings from Chinese Communists, Stalin remained blind to Chiang's true objectives. Then, in April, 1927, Kuomintang forces suddenly turned on their Communist allies and massacred them by the thousands. Thereafter Soviet influence was non-existent not only in Kuomintang China, but also with the Chinese

Communist Party which, under the leadership of Mao Tse-tung would henceforth pay lip service to Russian leadership, but ignore it at every decisive turn.

The central directorship of Communist parties throughout the world was lodged in the Comintern ("Communist International"), with headquarters in Moscow. Set up at the Third Communist International meeting in Moscow in 1919, the Comintern was no more nor less than a secondary Russian foreign office. Its directives to foreign Parties were carefully calculated to serve Russia's international interests first, and the local interests of foreign Communists second. For example, in Germany during the late twenties, the Communists, on instructions from the Comintern, devoted all their energies to fighting against German Socialists and Social-Democrats, not against Hitler. This reflected both Stalin's obsessive fear of competing leftist movements, and a haphazard theory that Germany would have to "go through" Nazism before it would be ripe for communism.

But with the rise of Nazism in Germany, fascism in Italy and militarism in Japan, it soon became clear to Russian leaders that their own nation had become target number one on a public timetable of conquest. Not without reason Stalin and his associates believed that influential circles in the capitalist democracies, England, France and the United States, hoped to use the Nazi-fascist barbarism as a weapon against the Soviet Union. Acting with that decisiveness possible to an absolute dictatorship, Stalin, in 1933-34, suddenly turned Russian foreign policy topsy-turvy. From then on cooperation became the by-word dutifully passed to foreign Communist Parties by the Comintern. Communists throughout the world were instructed to form "Popular Fronts" with those groups in any country who could be enlisted to fight the growing menace of Nazi-fascist expansionism. The Popular Fronts were intended to put pressure on their respective governments to reach economic and military agreements with the Soviet Union to present a common front against the new enemy.

Without doubt the high point of Popular Front activities came during the Spanish Civil War. When Spanish Fascists, under the leadership of General Francisco Franco, rose in rebellion against the Republican Government in Spain, the Comintern tried desperately to enlist world-wide support for the Republic. Almost alone among the nations, Russia poured advisors, technicians, planes, pilots, tanks and munitions into Spanish Republican ports. And to frustrated liberals in Britain, France or the United States, it seemed for a while that Communist interpretations were correct. The capitalist democracies seemed willing to let Spain fall into Fascist hands without a struggle; only the Soviet Union fought for true democracy. By hundreds of thousands, young men the world over volunteered to join the International Brigades, organized and equipped by local Communist Parties subordinate to the Comintern. They fought heroically in Spain—saving Madrid in 1936, defeating the Italians at Brunete in 1937. But their idealism was wasted. For Stalin had no interest in a Republican victory. Whenever it seemed that the Republic might score a decisive success,

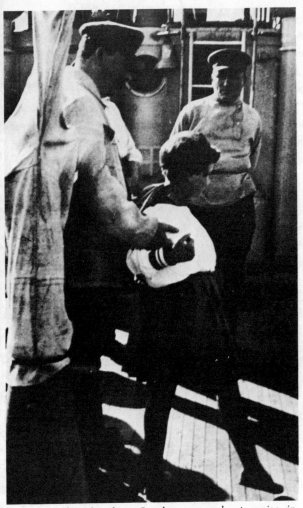

Stalin and his daughter Svetlana on a boat cruise in the Black Sea. Photograph was first published in 1967.

the flow of Russian supplies dwindled. On the other hand, when it seemed that the Republic could not long survive, another transfusion of arms would arrive from Moscow. In effect Stalin's main interest was in *prolonging* the war. For it made not only a brilliant propaganda spectacle, and tied up German and Italian forces, but there was also the chance that it might produce that accidental spark which could plunge England and France into war against

A Soviet ship arrives in Barcelona with food supplies for the anti-fascist forces in the Spanish Civil War.

Germany and Italy. For if certain western leaders hoped to turn Hitler east, Stalin hoped to turn him west. When, in 1939, Stalin allowed the Spanish Republic to die, it was the first sign of a coming change in Russian foreign policy. Other signs were the murders and imprisonments carried out against those Russians who had fought in Spain almost as soon as they returned to their homeland.

By 1939, with the capitulation of the democracies before Hitler's growing power evidenced in the German seizure of Austria, the re-militarization of the Rhineland, and finally, the dismemberment of Czechoslovakia, Stalin had come to believe that the west was not serious in its proclaimed opposition to German expansionism. In this he was at least partly right. Many in the west continued to hope blindly that somehow or other Hitler could be encouraged to unleash his armies east. In such a situation its was obvious, especially to a former Georgian bandit, that Hitler would accept the best bargain he could get. He got it, in total secrecy and with embarrassing haste, from Stalin. The Nazi-Soviet Pact of August, 1939, stupefied the world. And in its wake thousands of foreign Communists were disillusioned, the Popular Front movement collapsed—and Hitler was given the assurance of his eastern flank which enabled him to plunge the world into its most catastrophic war.

What was surprising was not that Stalin and Hitler had reached an understanding but that in the following months, Stalin placed such heavy reliance upon it. Evidently he really believed in German promises and Hitler's pledges. In any event, the pact was profitable. Now Poland was once again partitioned between Germany and Russia for the fourth time in her bloody history; the Baltic states—Lithuania, Latvia and Esthonia—were re-incorporated into the Soviet Union after their twenty-year taste of freedom. And a mismanaged but ultimately successful war against Finland in 1940 gave Russia control over the northern approaches to Leningrad. As Hitler's armies overran France, as the Luftwaffe battered England, Russian supplies of oil, wheat, clothing and food poured into Germany—along with congratulatory telegrams from Stalin for each German success. During the winter of 1940-1941, Soviet Foreign Minister Vyacheslav Molotov held several meetings with German Foreign Minister Joachim Ribbentrop. At one of which, they huddled in a Berlin bomb shelter while Ribbentrop offered to divide the entire world with Russia. The irony of the situation was not lost on Molotov who, when assured that Britain was already defeated, demanded: "Then why are we in this bomb shelter and whose are those bombs which are falling?" Nonetheless, Russian confidence in their new ally remained unshaken. Warnings about German troop concentrations in the Balkans, dispatched by Winston Churchill and President Franklin D. Roosevelt, were dismissed as "capitalist warmongering." No new dispositions were made of Red Army divisions, nor was any state of preparation embarked upon. Stalin and his associates continued to peer at the world from behind the secure walls of the Kremlin. Until June 22, 1941.

Dimitrov, Stalin, Molotov, Mikoyan and Chubar on the Kremlin reviewing stand for the 1937 May Day Parade.

1939 Nazi-Soviet Alliance. Joachim von Ribbentrop, Stalin and Molotov conclude their non-aggression pact.

WORLD
WAR II

"AND NO NATION IN THE HISTORY OF BATTLE EVER SUFFERED MORE THAN THE RUSSIANS SUFFERED IN THE COURSE OF THE SECOND WORLD WAR. ...AT LEAST TWENTY MILLION LOST THEIR LIVES. COUNTLESS MILLIONS OF HOMES AND FARMS WERE BURNED OR SACKED. A THIRD OF THE NATION'S TERRITORY, INCLUDING NEARLY TWO-THIRDS OF ITS INDUSTRIAL BASE, WERE TURNED INTO A WASTELAND."

AMERICAN UNIVERSITY IN WASHINGTON, D.C., JUNE 10, 1963.

June 22, 1941—*Adolf Hitler invades Russia. Nazi machine gunners attack western Russian villages and cities.*

Red Army tanks lie in ruins while German shock troops swarm through villages deserted by their inhabitants.

Camouflaged German anti-tank guns attack a nest of
Soviets cornered on the other side of the Dniester River.

Nazi Marshal Hermann Goering inspects captured lands.

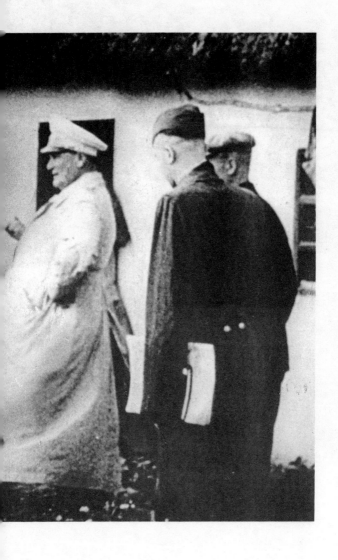

Hitler advances. And outside Moscow, women dig trenches.

The youth of Leningrad prepare to fight for their city.

Encircled and besieged by the Germans, every Leningrader fights back. Even women must learn trench warfare.

In September, 1941, three million Leningraders are totally cut off by the Germans from the rest of the country. Transportation halts, and only sleds travel the streets.

One-third of the population of Leningrad starves to death in the longest siege ever endured by a modern city.

But in heatless buildings life goes on. High-school students wear coats in the classroom to study physics.

A few supply trucks managed to reach Leningrad over frozen Lake Ladoga. But some fell through the weak ice.

Ukrainians welcome the German conquerors. Or so the German censor claimed when he released these photos.

Ukrainians imprisoned by the Germans are less pleased.

Russian children peer out of a Nazi concentration camp.

The Russian Jews. Here only two bodies remain unburned.

Russian slave labor plows the scorched Ukrainian earth.

A Russian church blazes after Nazi tanks have passed.

Stalingrad, 1942—German infantry approach the city.

Fighting inside a large factory in Stalingrad—1942.

Stalingrad during the fighting. The Russian Army and people were forced to defend their homes room by room.

A group of Russians celebrates the liberation of Stalingrad from the Germans. Scores of thousands lie dead.

169

The turning point of the war—February, 1943. The Red
Army had captured or destroyed twenty-two German Army
divisions at the conclusion of the Battle of Stalingrad.

Germans fall as the Red Army at last begins to advance.

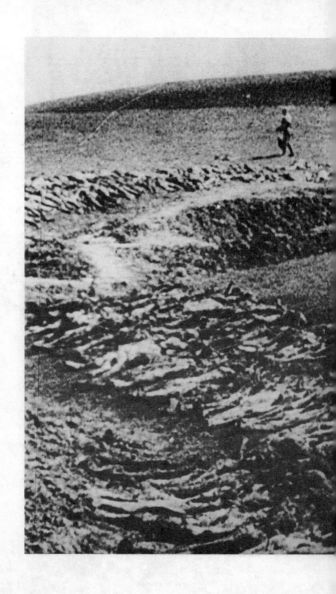

At Babi Yar, outside Kiev, lie the corpses of tens of thousands of Jews systematically murdered by the Nazis.

Teheran Conference, December, 1943. Stalin, Roosevelt and Churchill meet together to plan the German defeat.

American fliers in conversation with Russian soldiers at a Flying Fortress base inside the Soviet Union.

Every Russian citizen had to fight this war. With sons fighting at the front, pensioners man factories.

The defeated German Army at last flees from Russia.

The citizens of Warsaw return to the rubble of their homes after Russians capture the city from the Nazis.

The Big Three Conference at Yalta in February, 1945.

Soviet tanks arrive on the streets of Vienna, Austria.

A Red Army soldier dances with an Austrian girl as the happy Viennese celebrate the Nazi defeat in May, 1945.

The American and Red Armies meet. A group of Soviet soldiers pose with American fighters who have just victoriously crossed the Elbe River in central Germany.

The Fall of Berlin—Red Army tanks passing beside a wall inscribed: "Berlin shall always remain German."

Soviet detachments plunge toward the bombed Reichstag.

The hammer and sickle goes up over the wreckage of Adolf Hitler's insane dream of a Thousand Year Reich.

The victors meet at Potsdam, Germany, in the summer of 1945—Joseph Stalin, Harry Truman and Winston Churchill.

Allied generals meet after the war is over—Field Marshal Montgomery, General Eisenhower and Marshal Zhukov.

Soviet leaders review the Victory parade in the Kremlin. Stalin is flanked by Viacheslav Molotov and Marshal Zhukov, a hero too popular for Stalin's comfort.

END OF A
REVOLUTION

TO THE VICTORS...

In the sudden silence which descended over Europe in May, 1945, the Russian people, whose sons stood on the Elbe and mounted guard in shattered Berlin, had reason for pride and sorrow. Pride because more than any other single factor, it was the heroism and sacrifices of the Red Army which had destroyed Hitler's mighty war machine. Despite the blunders with which Stalin had begun the war, despite the massive incompetence demonstrated from time to time by the bureaucrats, Russian soldiers had won the greatest victory in world history. Sorrow because of the cost. An estimated twenty-five million Russians had been killed, both soldiers and civilians. Untold millions more returned to their villages in the wake of the Red Army to find only ruins. Great industrial centers, built at such a terrible price in human suffering, had been ground to dust. The Dniepropetrovsk dam, symbol of all that the new Russia had hoped for, had been destroyed as part of the scorched earth campaign before the oncoming Germans. The farm

Russian people demonstrate in a Moscow May Day parade.

Posters on a Kiev ruin try to recruit factory workers. So many people died during the war that there is a severe shortage of labor for rebuilding the Soviet Union.

animal population of the Soviet Union had been reduced to less than half its pre-war total; the nation's railways had been wrecked, its motor transport now consisted almost exclusively of American Lend-Lease vehicles. In large areas famine and the spectre of starvation stalked the land.

But there was reason for hope too. For the world into which a victorious Soviet Union emerged in 1945 offered promise of change, both at home and abroad. The Russian people had fought the war as a patriotic fatherland war, not as a Communist war. Stalin's policy of "Socialism in one country" had, during the immediate pre-war years, merged almost imperceptibly into a sort of state social-ism. With the onslaught of war it became outright na-tionalism. In speeches to the Russian people, during the conflict, Stalin himself emphasized the heroic Russian past—even though that could mean only the Czarist past. In November, 1941, for example, when he wanted to rouse the people of Moscow to defend the city, Stalin did not allude to Lenin or Marx or other Communist heroes, but rather to the "virile images of our great ancestors—Nevsky, Donskoy, Minin, Pozharsky, Suvorov and Kutuzov." Of these the first was a saint and the last two Czarist generals. Furthermore, at the insistence of Eng-land and the United States, Stalin had disbanded the Comintern in 1943. He had also paid public homage to the freedoms enshrined in such documents as the Atlantic Charter, and had joined the United Nations willingly enough. All this, to some Russians, presaged a possible relaxation of the dictatorship at home, of the terrible tensions under which they had now been living for thirty years. But such optimists reckoned without the deepening malaise of fear and suspicion which enveloped the Kremlin.

To Stalin and his associates, certain objective opportunities now presented themselves at the war's end, and they seized upon them as Russian nationalists, not as Communists. Russian troops had conquered all of eastern Europe. They had regained and passed beyond the old Czarist boundaries of Russia which had been lost in 1918. Just as any Russian government would have, Stalin's determined that these boundaries were now to be restored. In addition, all those nations of Eastern Europe— Poland, Czechoslovakia, Bulgaria, Romania and Hungary —which had during the twenties been formed by France into a "cordon sanitaire" *against* Bolshevik power, were now to become client states of the Soviet Union, under as absolute control as Moscow wished to exercise. Furthermore, as much as possible of Russia's losses during the war were to be regained by the confiscation of factories in the conquered lands, especially Germany. An estimated 36% of Germany's 1936 industrial capacity was shipped to Russia from East Germany immediately after the war. From all of Eastern Europe the spoils flowed to the victor.

England and the United States, eager to keep Russia fighting during the darker days of the war, and eager for Russian cooperation in the continuing struggle against Japan, had, at Teheran and later at Yalta, agreed that Eastern Europe, with the exception of Greece, might be

Ukrainian peasants reap a harvest from the resown land, although elsewhere many Russians are still starving.

A park of war trophies—Nazi planes captured by Soviets.

People rebuild their streets from the rubble of the war.

considered a Russian "sphere of influence." Further, those former Czarist regions of east Asia lost by Nicholas II were to be returned to his heirs. But the words "sphere of influence" did not mean to western diplomats what they meant in the Kremlin. Roosevelt, almost up to his death, evidently expected the Russians to sponsor free and open elections in Poland, Bulgaria and other Eastern European nations. Elections were held, but under the guns of the Red Army and the watchful eyes of political commissars sent out from Moscow. The West considered the Communist take-over in Eastern Europe to be a breach of faith; the Kremlin considered it the rightful spoils of war. This was the crux of the disagreements first evidenced between Truman and Stalin at the Potsdam Conference in 1945.

But there were deeper currents running in Stalin's mind which boded ill for the future. American and English cooperation with Russia during the war had made the Soviet dictator more mistrustful than ever. The enormous industrial potential of the United States, revealed by the American war effort, was frightening. When this was capped by the American production of atomic bombs (a fact of which Stalin was kept in ignorance until the first bomb ignited the sky above Hiroshima), Stalin suddenly realized that there was but one super-power in the world — and it was not Russia. The mindless saber-rattling of certain American generals and "public figures" did little to allay the normally suspicious minds in the Kremlin. Once more Stalin felt himself besieged. And he reacted in the coming years as he had reacted in the past.

THE IRON CURTAIN

Was it intended to keep foreigners out or Russians in? Both, but especially the latter. When Winston Churchill, at Fulton, Missouri, observed that "an iron curtain has settled across Europe," most Americans assumed he was referring to the impenetrability of the new Soviet empire to outsiders, especially westerners. But Russia, even under the Czars, had never been easy for foreigners to penetrate. Now the Russian borders had, in effect, been drawn to include all of Eastern Europe, and behind the occupying lines of the Red Army, nations familiar to the West (some, like Poland, with sizable blocs of American descendants) were completely cut off. The division of Europe between East and West was formalized during the summer of 1947 when Russia and her satellite states refused Marshall Plan aid and formed their own economic bloc.

But from the other side of the Iron Curtain, it looked remarkably like the old walls of suspicion which had long kept Russians from free access to the West. In re-

An American convoy enters the U.S. sector of Berlin. Surprisingly, the Russians allow it through their zone.

nouncing American aid, the Kremlin trotted out the old
dogmas of "capitalistic exploitation" and "dollar imperialism." That this was not entirely without justifica-
tion was demonstrated by the course of American aid to
Europe in subsequent years. One way and another, private American interests *did* wind up controlling a large
share of Western European capital investment. But to
Soviet citizens, the rejection of United States aid, even
with its disguised strings, meant a return to the austerity
and sacrifice of the early Five Year Plans. Despite the
looting of Eastern Europe—and, after Russia's successful
two-week war against Japan, of Manchuria—much Soviet
industry had to be rebuilt from scratch. A whole series
of new Five Year Plans were announced by Moscow.

The Stalinization of Eastern Europe—Albanian students parade at a Communist peace festival in East Germany.

And, like their earlier models, they concentrated all energies to the construction and rehabilitation of basic heavy industries. Little or nothing was left over for the production of those consumer goods for which Russians had been starved for generations. If there had been, it would have been swallowed anyhow by the additional new and urgent devotion of resources to develop an atomic bomb. Today the manufacture of atomic weapons has been somewhat simplified. But during the late forties and early fifties it required a vast and extremely sophisticated industrial establishment to produce them. The fact that observers of Russia had long pointed to the excellence of Russia's technical education program, to the large numbers of first-rate engineers being gradu-

West Berliners watch American planes airlift food and
supplies to them over the Communist blockade in 1948.

ated yearly from Russian universities, did not prepare the West, especially the United States, for the shock of Russia's speedy development of atomic weapons and for the explosion of the first Soviet hydrogen bomb in 1953 The success of Soviet atomic development was a good indication of the general success of the program to re-build Russian industry.

Not only were Russians re-enlisted after the war into a new series of sacrificial Five Year Plans, but they were also enlisted into a revival of the Communist ideological crusade at home and abroad. During the war, millions of Russian soldiers had glimpsed for themselves the eco-nomic "wonders" of some of the countries they had con-quered. Amusing stories of the bafflement with which Siberian troops regarded such devices as bathtubs, toilets and water-taps were not entirely unfounded. Moreover, many Russian officers and administrators had had pro-longed contact with Allied officials. To Kremlin minds, these soldiers and officials were potential germ-bearers to their native land; the germ being doubt of the infallible wisdom of Moscow's interpretations and decrees. To counteract any such epidemic of thought, Stalin un-leashed a new barrage of Communist conformism upon the Russian people. The United States and Britain, only recently "gallant democratic allies," were now pictured as "imperialist hyenas." The western contribution to Russian defense through Lend Lease, and to the defeat of Hitlerism, was played down in official histories until it had all but disappeared. Nationalism, which had been purposely generated as a morale factor during the war, was now pushed to hysterical extremes as Russians were discovered to have invented everything from the steam-engine to penicillin. Conformity to Marxist theory, as interpreted by Stalin, was demanded in every field, from art to physics. Immense intellectual energies were expended to twist intransigent scientific fact into an acceptable Communist mold. Perhaps the most notorious demonstration of the regime's intellectual censorship came in 1948 when the biological theories of Trofim Lysenko (whose doctrine of the inheritance of acquired characteristics in plants seemed hopeful proof that new generations of Russians might actually be born with a predisposition towards communism) were declared to be state doctrine. Foreign biologists who scoffed at Lysenko's findings were officially ridiculed; Soviet scientists who questioned them were treated as heretics. The new Soviet metaphysics was decisively enthroned in every area of thought.

While the Soviet crusade of Communist-nationalism reached new heights at home, the Russian crusade of Communist-internationalism was re-instituted abroad. The defunct Comintern was brought back into existence in 1947 as the Cominform ("Communist Information Bureau"). Its functions not only included the fomentation of trouble in capitalist lands and the direction of foreign Communist parties according to Moscow's international needs, but now it was the agency through which political control was exercised in the captive states of Eastern Europe. That such control was more dependent upon the presence of the Red Army than on the effectiveness of

Cominform exhortation was demonstrated by Yugoslavian dictator Tito's successful defiance of Cominform directives in 1948, which led to the first apparent split in the supposedly monolithic Communist power structure.

Nor could Soviet leaders claim credit for the success of Mao Tse-tung's successful revolutionary war in China. Russians were deluged with Moscow's self-congratulations on the Communist conquest of China, but the truth was that despite some Russian aid in Manchuria, Mao's decades-long struggle against Nationalist China was strictly indigenous. During the thirties, the Chinese Communist Party had received nothing but advice from the Kremlin (which it usually ignored); during World War II Russia actively supported Chiang Kai-shek and even sent him what supplies it could. When in 1949 Chinese Communist troops marched into Shanghai, they were equipped with American guns, tanks and trucks which

Stalin-Allee, built as a showplace street in East Berlin after the war. Behind the buildings — war rubble.

they had captured from Nationalist divisions, not Russian. Of course, with Mao's victory, Soviet advisors and industrial aid began to pour into China. But if the men in the Kremlin assumed that Mao had reason to be grateful to them, or that as the "senior partners" of world communism their leadership would remain unquestioned by him, they were badly mistaken.

The Iron Curtain undoubtedly had its external uses. But primarily it was another measure of control on the Russians themselves, imposed by the increasingly suspicious, increasingly insecure mind of a paranoiac dictator. Whenever that control was threatened, Stalin responded with increased force. And in the complex world of the fifties, his control was increasingly threatened.

Stalin's body lies in state within the Kremlin walls.

Stalin's pallbearers—(left to right) Bulganin (with white goatee), Molotov, Stalin's son Vassily, the new Premier Malenkov, and chief of the secret police Beria.

Industrial reconstruction had been a success, but at a terrible human price. The new technical elite, indispensable to Russian scientific and economic development, were showing increasing signs of restiveness. Soviet power abroad, as the case of Yugoslavia demonstrated, had its limits. And Soviet intervention abroad had been contained in Greece in 1947 by the Truman Doctrine. In Korea (1950-53) American and United Nations troops inflicted a stunning defeat on Russian-sponsored North Korean invading forces.

Responding to new threats, both real and imaginary, Stalin evidently prepared for a new Great Purge in late 1952. On March 15, 1952, Laurenti P. Beria, Minister of the Interior and former boss of the dreaded NKVD, was once again appointed head of the secret police, now known as the MGB. In October, at the 19th Party Congress held in Moscow, Stalin replaced the old eleven-man Politburo, with whom he had shared power, with a new Presidium, much expanded and including many new faces. The men around the dictator, according to their own later testimony, began to feel the cold winds of imprisonment and murder. In January, 1953, nine doctors and professors of medicine (some of whom had been attending the ailing Stalin) were suddenly arrested and charged with conspiracy to poison top Soviet officials. This fantastic accusation was, to those who knew Stalin best, the signal for a new reign of terror. And then, suddenly, on March 5, 1953, seventy-three-year-old Joseph Vissarionovich Dzhugashvili died of a massive brain hemorrhage.

DE-STALINIZATION

To the men around the old dictator, his death must have come as something of a deliverance. Some, at least, felt themselves slated for liquidation, and now they moved quickly to save themselves. Only two days after Stalin's death, the new thirty-six-man Presidium was reduced once again to ten members. Georgi Malenkov, Stalin's Deputy Premier and former Director of War Production, became Premier. Nikita Khrushchev took over as First Secretary of the Communist Party. The old Stalinists, Vyacheslav Molotov, Lazar Kaganovich and Nikolai Bulganin, remained at their posts, as did the sinister Laurenti Beria, Minister of the Interior. Stalin was buried, amid all the circumstances of Communist pomp, alongside the mummified corpse of Lenin in the mausoleum outside the Kremlin walls. To a world which had no means of penetrating the reality of the Soviet transfer of power, it appeared at first that things would go on as they had.

The first sign of a change in the domestic atmosphere was a strike by the slave laborers at the infamous

Lenin and Stalin marbleized—a partnership soon to disappear from sculpture and portraiture in the Soviet Union.

Vorkuta slave labor camp on the Arctic Circle. In the past such a demonstration would have been silenced with machine guns. But now, to the wonderment of those few Soviet citizens aware of the facts, the strikers were not murdered. In fact many of their demands for better housing and food were met. The next sign was the sudden arrest of Laurenti Beria and six of his top assistants in June, 1953. They were tried and executed in less than two weeks, presumably for using the MGB, and the NKVD before it, for personal vengeances. Thereafter the MGB was reorganized into the KGB and many of its powers abrogated. Beginning in 1953, a series of sweeping amnesties were issued by the new government which freed approximately two-thirds of the five million political and common criminals still languishing in Russian prisons and labor camps. Thereafter the labor camps were closed.

On the international front, the change of direction was signaled by the renewal of truce talks in Korea and the abrupt decision to accept U.N. terms for the exchange of prisoners of war in the spring of 1953. And in the next two years the world became accustomed to the "goodwill" visits of Malenkov and Bulganin, looking somewhat like benign bears, in such unlikely capitals as London and Cairo. Talks were initiated with the United States looking towards an easing of tensions.

But the power struggle in the Kremlin was not yet over. Stalin's death had left an inviting vacuum which was but uneasily filled by the ten members of the Presidium. So far, however, none of them had felt himself strong enough to take over the old dictator's commanding role. But Nikita Khrushchev made as good use of his First Secretaryship of the Party as had Stalin decades earlier. By 1955 he had sufficient strength to force Malenkov from the Premiership and to replace him with Bulganin.

Then, in February, 1956, at the Twentieth Party Congress during a secret session, Khrushchev exploded a bombshell. With obvious authority (he had worked with Stalin for years) and in great detail, he launched an all-out attack upon Stalin's memory. He accused the dead dictator of megalomania, sadism, cowardice and incompetence. Obviously overcome by bitter emotions, Khrushchev talked for six hours—and every word exploded the mythical world that devout Communists had inhabited for decades. Now it seemed that all those who had fallen victims to the Great Purges of the late thirties had been innocent; all the millions of peasants who perished from starvation during the twenties had been victims of stupidity; the intellectuals who had been hounded and imprisoned after World War II had suffered for one man's paranoia. In short, Nikita Khrushchev, First Secretary of the Communist Party and an intimate of Joseph Stalin's for many years, publicly admitted most of the charges against his former leader which had long been advanced by the bitterest foreign critics of the Soviet regime. The effects were immediate and startling.

First, several foreign Communist Parties assumed that since the new Soviet government had condemned Stalinist tactics, they would be freer to pursue their own national paths. The workers' riots in Poznan, Poland in

*Nicholas Bulganin, Communist Party Secretary Khrushchev,
Premier Malenkov—The new leaders of the Soviet Union.*

Khrushchev and Malenkov pay a visit to a collective farm.

Khrushchev appears to charm Chinese leader Mao Tse-tung.

Khrushchev announces Malenkov's resignation, with the latter at his side. Now in total command, he makes his famous denunciation of Stalin not long afterward.

Encouraged by de-Stalinization in Russia, Hungarians rise in rebellion against their Communist leadership.

June, 1956, and the Hungarian uprising in the autumn of that same year, were both directly inspired by hopes generated by Khrushchev's speech. But the savagery and bloodshed with which both revolts were crushed showed that no matter how far the new masters of the Kremlin were prepared to relax the domestic stringency of Stalinism, they were not prepared to abandon Russia's permanent geo-political interests in central Europe.

A second result of the anti-Stalin speech was the formation of an anti-Khrushchev group on the Soviet Presidium. Even today it is uncertain how much clearance Khrushchev had obtained for his speech. Certainly Molotov, Kaganovich and Malenkov—all of whom had shared Stalin's glory and would presumably have to share his new obloquy—could not have welcomed such a violent exposure of the past. In any event they now opposed Khrushchev, just as Lenin's old associates had once opposed Stalin. In June, 1957, all three men were expelled from the Presidium—not this time to liquidation, but simply to the humiliation of obscure posts in the giant Soviet bureaucracy. In March, 1958, Bulganin, who had supported the ousted members, was forced from his post as Premier in favor of Khrushchev. Now, five years after Stalin's death, all his powers were once again concentrated in the hands of one man—Nikita Khrushchev.

Whatever his skills as a politician (and they must have been considerable), Khrushchev also had a positive program to present to the Russian people and to the Soviet government. In 1957 he pushed through a massive decentralization of the economic controls centered in the Moscow bureaucracy. The Soviet Union was divided into over 100 regions for administrative purposes. Each region was henceforth to be governed by economic decisions taken by its own local Soviet. It was hoped thus to eliminate red tape, pacify the increasing demand for local autonomy and increase the efficiency of the industrial plant.

But even beyond his new programs, Khrushchev was offering himself as a leader and symbol for a new era in Soviet history. The Russian people who had little choice in the matter seized upon him as such, and new liberal tendencies gained a momentum which they have not yet lost.

The Red Army quickly smashes Hungarian hopes, although Stalin's statue topples in Budapest, never again to rise.

THE THAW AND THE ICE AGE

Ever alert to tactical changes in Russian policy which might give ground for optimism, the western world hailed Stalin's downfall and the evidence of more liberal domestic policies as signs of a "thawing out" of the Cold War between the USSR and the USA. Soviet repression of the Poznan and Hungarian uprisings was dismissed as "necessity." The signing of a Cultural Exchange Pact with the United States in 1956, the visit of Khrushchev to the United States in 1957 (what would Lenin, Trotsky or Stalin have made of that photo of the burly Soviet leader sitting down to dinner with tuxedoed American millionaires in San Francisco?), the much touted "spirit of Camp David"—all these symptoms were greeted as the beginning of the end of Russian hostility to the West.

They were, in fact, symbols of an easing of *Communist* dogmas of hate toward the "rotten capitalist democracies." But behind the Communist line lay always the real and ever-present needs of specifically Russian national policy. Where Russian and American ambitions and in-

A thaw in Russia? Khrushchev visits the United States
twice, and meets with President Kennedy in Vienna.

Meanwhile in Berlin a Communist wall divides the city.

Nikita Khrushchev ships missiles to Fidel Castro's Cuba.

1962—The United States blockades Cuba and the Soviet Union backs down during the world-shaking crisis.

terests clashed, there would be conflict irrespective of political or economic theory. One such area of conflict was Germany. Russia, which had suffered cruelly from two German invasions within twenty-five years, was determined that Germany never again find the power to renew its *Drang Nach Osten*. It must remain divided or totally disarmed. But the United States, seeing in Germany its only reliable source of manpower and eco-

nomic power with which to prop up the NATO alliance against Russian ambitions in western Europe, proceeded to re-arm a new generation of Germans. Thus, although the bald insult of the U-2 reconnaissance plane incursions over Soviet territory was seized upon by Khrushchev in 1958 to disrupt the Paris Summit Conference and to dispel the friendly vapors of the "spirit of Camp David," there remained more significant and permanent causes for conflict between the world's two super-powers. The various manufactured Berlin crises, especially those of 1958 and 1961 when the Great Wall of communism was erected, reflected the continuing divergence of American and Russian aims in Germany.

Nor was there any doubt now that Russia was truly a super-power. The faintly idiotic western jeering about "socialist inefficiency" was silenced in 1957 when the Soviets, beating the Americans into space, launched their first Sputnik. The continuing demonstration of Soviet technological prowess and scientific advance was symbolized by the fact that the first man in space in 1961 was a Russian, not an American.

But the most significant change in Russia's international position was to take place not in its relations with the west, but in its relations with Red China. Following

The Russian-Chinese split. Chinese students demonstrate in Moscow and struggle with the Russian police.

almost immediately upon the heels of Khrushchev's anti-Stalin speech in 1956 was a noticeable deterioration in Sino-Russian relations. Accusing the Kremlin of "cowardice" in its policy towards the United States, Mao Tse-tung's Chinese Communist Party undertook an increasing campaign of vilification against Moscow. Russian advisors and technicians were expelled from China and, conversely, Russian aid ceased. Aside from those permanent geo-political causes of friction which had kept the long Sino-Russian borders in a state of tension since the time of Czar Nicholas, the new battle of slogans, insults and petty annoyances waged against Russia by Red China was significant of a basic change in Russian foreign policy. Impressed by the tremendous power of nuclear weapons and long-range rockets now at their disposal, Khrushchev and his associates, like their American counterparts, had more or less abandoned the idea that any possible gains in an all-out war with the United States could ever counter-balance the world-wide destruction such a conflict would entail. Russian arms and advisors would continue to pour into those nations whose successful national liberation wars showed promise of embarrassing or undermining western power (Algeria, Egypt, Cuba). But no foreign adventures were likely to be pressed to the point of full-scale war. Likewise, American arms and troops might be used to preserve western domination in certain areas (The Dominican Republic, Lebanon, South Viet Nam), but Washington showed no disposition to precipitate a suicidal war against the

Soviet Union. The miscalculations which brought both nations to the brink of disaster over Cuba in 1962 (the American-sponsored abortive Bay of Pigs invasion, the Russian-sponsored installation of ballistic missiles) dramatized both the terrible dangers of war and the determination of both countries to avoid it.

Beyond the realization that power has its limits in the nuclear age, the Kremlin's new leaders seem to have arrived at the conclusion that the world-wide Communist crusade would have to take second or third place in the scheme of Soviet priorities—behind efforts to improve living standards in Russia itself. Much of the aggressive dynamism of Moscow's proselytizing seemed to have evaporated in a growing realization that the world was far too complex for any single system of political or economic metaphysics. So when Mao Tse-tung accused the Kremlin of "softness," of "revisionism," of "abandonment of the principles of Marxism-Leninism," he was speaking the truth.

The real significance of the Sino-Russian quarrel may well be that it signifies the beginning of the end of Soviet attempts to export their revolution to countries in which it is not welcomed. The "thaw" in Russian attitudes to the outside world may be but a passing phenomenon (and much depends on the American response to it). Or, hopefully, it may mark the first signs that the fifty-year ice age of Soviet foreign relations is drawing to a close. Whatever its international significance, it reflects very real and basic changes in the nature of Soviet society.

THE ORGANIZATION MEN

At the 22nd Party Congress held in Moscow in 1961, Nikita Khrushchev called for a new series of economic plans. But unlike the old Five Year Plans, these new programs were aimed less toward development of basic industry than toward the production of consumer goods and services. An increase of 500% in industrial production and of 250% in agricultural production was called for, to be achieved in the space of twenty years. The publicly proclaimed aims of the new plans were to surpass the United States in the production of *all* manufactured goods and to give Soviet citizens the world's highest standard of living. These aims and their implicit confession that the Soviet Union was not yet paradise for its citizens would have been anathema to Stalin for they seemed to substitute a quest for comfort for the expansion of power. But they most probably reflected the new climate of Soviet life very accurately.

During the years of intensive education, of the construction of a new and complex industrial society in

An obelisk crowned with a rocket symbolizes the Soviet Union's achievements in the exploration of outer space.

Russia, the emergence of a new hierarchy of technicians and managers was unavoidable. To technicians with years of intensive university study, used to the disciplines of free inquiry within their respective fields, the imposition of Marxist dogmas in other realms of thought had grown increasingly irrelevant, if not distasteful. The managers of the Soviet economy, incorporated into the vast government bureaucracy (it is presently estimated to include 20 million people), had grown increasingly conservative. They were much more interested in preserving their own places in the hierarchy and in improving their personal chances for promotion than in applying Marxist metaphysics to real and present problems of production and organization. Within the class of technicians and managers the *militancy* of Communist idealism had definitely declined. By the 1960's, the chief work of Marxist theoreticians in the Soviet Union seemed to be the torturing of Marxist doctrine to fit the new attitudes, rather than criticizing the new attitudes in the light of Marxist doctrine.

Furthermore, even during the bleak days of the Stalinist Five Year Plans, technicians and managers had been set apart from the ordinary people. They were paid higher wages, their children went to better schools, they received such perquisites as automobiles, country houses, better rations and even, on the more exalted levels, servants. Despite the terrors of the Stalinist purges, a definite tendency towards the creation of an upper and a middle class in the Soviet "classless society" was discernible even before World War II. With the end of the war and, especially, with the end of Stalinism, the tendency became an established fact. The Soviet Union now had a numerous class of people with a large personal investment in stability, comfort and peace.

With the liberalization of the regime and its increasing devotion to filling the private needs of its citizens, the ranks of the new middle and upper classes rapidly broadened. Above all, workers and collective farmers were encouraged to believe that their individual standard of living could and would be elevated to a level of very real prosperity. Something like a "revolution of rising expectations" seems to have taken place. To be sure, lip-service to Communist doctrine is still paid by the devout, but there are clear indications that among the masses, as among their rulers, revolutionary dogma must now wait upon the "good life."

Not that the good life is just around the corner. The heady goals set by Khrushchev in 1961 had to be somewhat modified in 1964 when new plans were adopted which placed the date of "surpassing the United States" in production into the indefinite future. But the Soviet Gross National Product has been rising at a rate between 5.5% and 6% per year since the fifties (compared with an average growth rate of 3.5% in the United States), and there is reason to believe that given continued peace, the Soviet Union will reach its goals during the next decades.

The desire for peace and stability, for "socialist legality" which now pervades a nation bone-weary of violence and fanaticism, was dramatically signaled by the

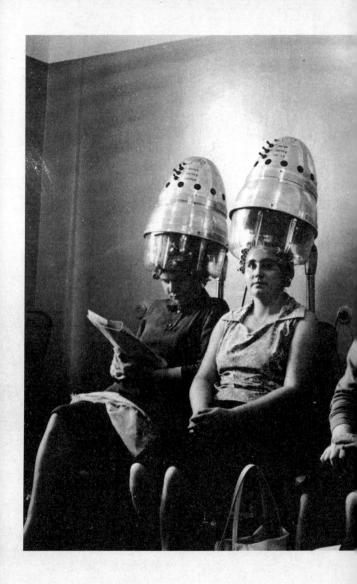

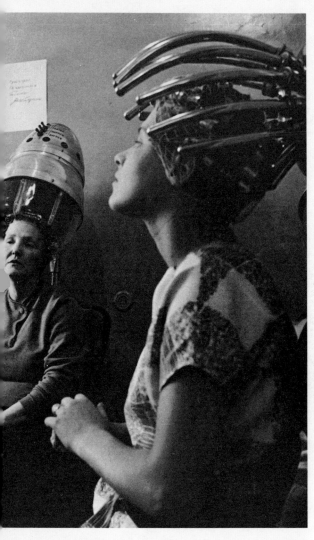

A Moscow beauty salon. Today the Soviet government places more emphasis on consumer needs and wishes.

Red Army military training camp in Soviet Russia today.

The popular and outspoken Russian poet Yevgeny Yev-
tushenko recites his poems for a Moscow audience.

downfall in 1964 of Nikita Khrushchev. Partly because
his 1961 plans had been over-optimistic, partly because
his decentralization schemes had not worked (in 1963 the
more than 100 new economically autonomous regions
had been reduced by more than half in the interest of
efficiency), and partly because his Cuban adventure had
misfired, the Premier and First Secretary was voted out
of office by his colleagues on the Presidium in late 1964.
No complex Byzantine intrigue seemed to be involved.

Certainly no punishment was meted out to the departing leader. He was simply and legally voted out of office and replaced by Leonid Brezhnev as First Secretary of the Communist Party and Aleksei Kosygin as Chairman of the Council of Ministers (Premier).

Aside from the legality and peacefulness of the transfer of power, the basic reasons for it were highly illuminating. Khrushchev was assailed in conference for having attempted to recreate the old "cult of personality" associated with Stalin. He was accused of disregarding the wishes both of the Presidium and of the Soviets. In short he was accused of acting too much like a dictator. His personality—rough (the shoe-pounding at the United Nations), effervescent (his exchange of jokes with American millionaires) and aggressive (his blustering interview with Kennedy in Vienna in 1961)—was simply not the image that the new managers of Soviet society wished to project to the outside world. Nikita Khrushchev was removed from power in the same way that the manager of any giant American corporation might be dismissed by dissatisfied stockholders and board members. Like a nineteenth-century "robber baron," he had become an anachronism in the complex world of the twentieth century and had lost control of his organization to the "organization men"—men whose sober faces and cautious words (as exemplified by Kosygin at Glassboro, New Jersey in 1967) were the very antithesis of the revolutionary zeal which had created their world.

The advent of the organization men, and of the forces which support them, certainly marks the end of the Russian revolution. But it by no means marks the end of that heroic struggle on the part of the Russian people, begun fifty years ago, to lift themselves into the modern world. The creation and preservation of the Soviet Union is one of the great permanent achievements of humanity on this planet. It has cost the Russian people dearly—in famine, despotism, war and anguish. But it is an accomplished fact and one for which the world, seeking peace and stability, may one day be grateful.

A gallery in Leningrad's famed and lovely Hermitage.

A rare ritual in modern Russia—the presentation of a new Torah to the one remaining synagogue in Odessa.

Only the old worship at this Russian Orthodox Church.

Young students at the Bolshoi Ballet School in Moscow.

The former star of the Bolshoi Ballet, Galina Ulanova.

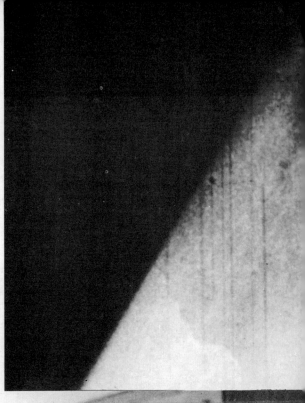

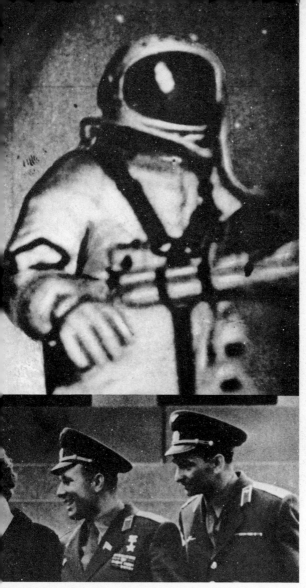

Cosmonaut Leonov walks in outer space. New Russian heroes—Cosmonauts Popovich, Nikolayev, Titov, Gagarin and Bykovsky surround Tereshkova, first lady in space.

The memory of Vladimir Lenin in a modern Russian home.

Brezhnev and Kosygin at the head of a familiar parade.

PHOTOGRAPH SOURCES

"A" indicates top of page; "B" and "C" indicate bottom.

HERMAN AXELBANK   13A/76/98-9/126/174-5

THE BETTMAN ARCHIVE   16/45/68-9/85/91B/94A

CHARLES PHELPS CUSHING   9/19/105A/160-61/
162-63A/180A/189A

EUROPEAN PICTURE SERVICE   35B/88-9/96-7/110/
113A/117A/142-3/144A/144B/148A/154A/155A/156A/
156B/157A/178A/202-3/220A/209

HISTORICAL PICTURES SERVICE—CHICAGO
58/71/72/80-1

MAGNUM   198A/Robert Capa 107/193/196-7/198B/
215/254-5/Erich Lessing 220/223A/H. Cartier-Bresson
226-7/252/Marc Riboud 238-9/Cornell Capa 245/248/
Elliott Erwitt 246A/Emmanuel D'Astier 133A

MUSEUM OF MODERN ART, STILLS ARCHIVE   32B

PICTORIAL PARADE   26A/26-7B/48-9/69/91A/92A/
210-11   (Paris Match)

PIX   28A/46 (Camera Press)

RAPHO-GUILLUMETTE   Christa Armstrong 190-1/
John Bryson 235/Caio Garruba 240-1/246-7

SOVFOTO   6-7/11/12/13B/20A/20B/23A/30-1/32A/
35A/40-1/43/46-7/51/53/56/57/61/62/64-5/68/75/77/
79/84A/84B/86/94-5A/102/105B/111/117B/118-9/121/
122-3/127/136/138-9/146-7/148B/149/150A/151A/
153A/152-3B/158-9A/158-9B/164-5B/166/167/168-9A/
169B/170-1/172/173/176B/177A/178-9/180B/181/
182-3/184A/184-5/186-7/188A/188-9B/212/218/219A/
219B/225/228/230-1/231B/242-3/249/250/251/253

UNITED PRESS INTERNATIONAL   129/201A

U.S. SIGNAL CORPS   82-3/86-7/96B

WIDE WORLD PHOTOS   25/35C/38-9/101/134/137/
145/164-5A/176A/204-5/222-3/229

Color photographs on covers by Bill Hofmann.
Black and white photos on back cover from Sovfoto,
Charles Phelps Cushing and Cornell Capa—Magnum.